Walt Whitman

Updated Edition

Twayne's United States Authors Series

David J. Nordloh, Editor

Indiana University at Bloomington

TUSAS 20

Steel engraving of a Daguerreotype of Whitman that appeared in the 1855 and some later editions of *Leaves of Grass*; Whitman said he considered it an integral part of the text of "Song of Myself."

Walt Whitman

Updated Edition

By James E. Miller, Jr.

University of Chicago

Twayne Publishers • Boston
A Division of G. K. Hall & Co.

Walt Whitman, Updated Edition
James E. Miller, Jr.

Copyright 1990 by G. K. Hall & Co.
All rights reserved.
Published by Twayne Publishers
A division of G. K. Hall & Co.
70 Lincoln Street
Boston, Massachusetts 02111

Copyediting supervised by Barbara Sutton.
Book production by Janet Z. Reynolds.
Book design by Barbara Anderson.
Typeset in 11 pt. Garamond
by Compset, Inc., Beverly, Massachusetts.

First published 1990.
10 9 8 7 6 5 4 3 2 1

Library of Congress Cataloging-in-Publication Data
Miller, James Edwin, 1920–
    Walt Whitman / by James E. Miller, Jr. — Updated ed.
        p.   cm. — (Twayne's United States authors series ; TUSAS 20)
    Includes bibliographical references (p.   )
    ISBN 0-8057-7600-1 (alk. paper)
    1. Whitman, Walt, 1819–1892—Criticism and interpretation.
I. Title.   II. Series.
PS3238.M57   1990
811'.3—dc20   89-24689
                                                                            CIP

To Kathleen Farley
Pennies from Heaven

I know I am solid and sound,
To me the converging objects of the universe perpetually flow,
All are written to me, and I must get what the writing means.

W. W.

Contents

About the Author

James E. Miller, Jr., is the Helen A. Regenstein Professor of Literature at the University of Chicago, where he has taught since 1962. In 1957 he published *A Critical Guide to "Leaves of Grass,"* which won the Walt Whitman Award of the Poetry Society of America. He edited the Houghton Mifflin Riverside Edition of Whitman's *Complete Poetry and Selected Prose* in 1959. He was coauthor in 1960 with Bernice Slote and Karl Shapiro of *Start with the Sun,* a book on the Whitman tradition of cosmic poetry that won the Poetry Chap-Book Award of the Poetry Society of America. And in 1979, he published *The American Quest for a Supreme Fiction: Whitman's Legacy in the Personal Epic.* He is also the author of *Quests Surd and Absurd: Essays in American Literature* (1967) as well as books on Herman Melville, F. Scott Fitzgerald, and J. D. Salinger. His *T. S. Eliot's Personal Waste Land: Exorcism of the Demons* appeared in 1977.

Miller received his B. A. from the University of Oklahoma and his M. A. and Ph.D. from the University of Chicago. He taught at the University of Nebraska, where he served as chair of the Department of English, a position he has also held at the University of Chicago. He has lectured in Australia and taught in Italy and Japan on Fulbright grants, and he has also taught at the Sorbonne in Paris. In 1970 he served as president of the National Council of Teachers of English, and in 1984 as president of the Association of Departments of English (of the Modern Language Association).

Preface

When the first edition of *Walt Whitman* appeared in 1962, over twenty-five years ago, Whitman was just emerging from under the dark cloud hung over him by the New Critics. In the time since, he has indeed come into his own, linked, for example, by respectable critics as a crucial predecessor poet to such a formidable modernist as Wallace Stevens. It is hard for me now to believe that when I first encountered Whitman's poetry as an undergraduate at the University of Oklahoma in 1939, it was a bowdlerized version of "Song of Myself" in the old Jones and Leisy anthology (*Major American Writers*) that excited me; or rather, it was the omitted parts that I discovered on my own that held me spellbound.

In his seminar on Whitman at the University of Chicago in 1948–49, Napier Wilt had difficulty finding a text of *Leaves of Grass* available for classroom use. I learned then that there were others who shared my enthusiasm—but I discovered, too, that many professors, critics, and poets sneered at Whitman. After I had begun to teach Whitman myself, in the early 1950s, I was amazed and enchanted when I came across Randall Jarrell's "Some Lines from Whitman" (1953): here was a poet who did a fireworks display by tossing up into the air a scattering of Whitman's great lines. By the time I was writing about Whitman, in the late 1950s, the Beats, wandering up and down America's open road, had appropriated Whitman as their guru-muse. Then I decided I needed no longer to despair about Whitman's place in American literature.

The intention of this book remains the same as before: to introduce Whitman to those who feel the need of such a formal meeting. As an introduction, the book has become something of both an end and a beginning. It is an end in that it has assimilated much of the mountain of material, scholarly and critical, that has accumulated about Whitman through the years. It is a beginning in that it suggests much and hints at more that only the reader can bring to completion by perusing the *Leaves*. Although this book remains, as it was in its first edition, indebted to much that has gone before, it is meant to be more than a synthesis. In intent, at least, its voice has remained singular and its view fresh.

The objective of this book is to provide as many entrances as possible to Whitman's poetry. Each chapter presents a way of beginning. First, Whitman the man is set forth in a series of vignettes revealing the various roles he assumed and the images he projected. The remainder of the book concentrates on his writing. Chapter 2 shows how the *Leaves* grew through some six lifetime editions; chapter 3 shows how the various prose works developed and gradually set forth a new poetics for the New World. Succeeding chapters treat a variety of facets of the *Leaves*—its final epic structure, its greatest individual poems, its recurring images, its language, wit, and wisdom. The last chapter sums up the distinctive quality of Whitman's genius as it may be detected in the bardic voice of his *Leaves*.

The revision has been detailed throughout, in the sentences, paragraphs, and chapters, but only with the purposes of correcting errors and bringing the bibliography and the frame of reference up to date. Whereas it was customary to refer to the nine editions of *Leaves of Grass* at the time of the first edition, we know now that strictly speaking there are only six, plus three "issues."[1] The Beat Generation's interest in Whitman has now given way to that of such groups as gay rights activists and feminists.

I would like to reaffirm my appreciation to those I acknowledged in the preface to the first edition: to Professors Napier Wilt and Gay Wilson Allen; to Mr. Charles Feinberg; to my colleagues then at the University of Nebraska, Bernice Slote, Karl Shapiro, and Bernard Kreissman; and to Sylvia Bowman, then editor of the Twayne United States Authors Series, who read the original manuscript with "meticulous care." Barbara Sutton has read the revised manuscript with similar care and discrimination. I learned much about Whitman from my seminars at both the University of Nebraska and the University of Chicago, and from my students who wrote dissertations on Whitman, including David Kuebrich and Kenneth Price. I am deeply grateful to Kathleen Farley, who did the spadework for this revision, who gave valuable advice, and who has been helpful at every turn in bringing it to the stage of publication.

I have continued to cite my Riverside Edition of Whitman, *Complete Poetry and Selected Prose*, which is based on the 1902 ten-volume *Complete Writings*. I have, however, checked other texts in order to be sure that the passages I cite are reliable. In most of the Whitman quotations, what look like ellipses points are usually his, used for rhetorical purposes; but on occasion I have indicated omission by such points. Readers who find the matter important should check the cited texts to resolve any questions.

After spending a lifetime reading, teaching, quoting, and writing about Whitman, and seeing his star gradually rise and its luster increase, I am delighted to bring an introductory book on him up to date. And I send it forth in the hope that in the next quarter century it will help lead new generations of readers into a personal perusal of that most powerful and astonishing of New World poems, *Leaves of Grass.*

James E. Miller, Jr.

University of Chicago

Chronology

1857–1859   Edits Brooklyn *Daily Times.*

1860   Goes to Boston to oversee publication of the third edition of *Leaves of Grass*; rejects Emerson's advice to exclude "Children of Adam" and other sex poems.

1861   Civil War begins. Whitman's Boston publisher fails, but the third edition continues to circulate through unauthorized use of the plates.

1862   Goes to Civil War battlefield in Virginia seeking wounded brother, George; finds brother recovering but many comrades maimed and suffering, needing help.

1863–1865   Becomes the "wound-dresser," visiting and tending the sick and injured in Washington; develops friendship with horse-car conductor Peter Doyle.

1865   Begins working in the Indian Bureau of the Department of Interior. Publishes *Drum-Taps*; adds "Lilacs" elegy as sequel after Lincoln's assassination in April. In June removed from one office because of his objectionable poems, but immediately appointed in the attorney general's office.

1866   W. D. O'Connor publishes *The Good Gray Poet,* defending Whitman from charge of obscenity.

1867   John Burroughs publishes *Walt Whitman as Poet and Person.* Fourth edition of *Leaves of Grass* published.

1868   William Michael Rossetti publishes selection of *Leaves* in England.

1869   Mrs. Anne Gilchrist reads Rossetti's edition of Whitman's poems, falls in love with him, and writes "An Englishwoman's Estimate of Walt Whitman" (published in the Boston *Radical Review* in 1870).

1871–1872   Publishes fifth edition of *Leaves of Grass, Democratic Vistas* (dated 1871), and *Passage to India* pamphlet, which is later included in a reissue of the fifth edition (dated 1872).

1873   Suffers paralytic stroke; mother dies; moves from Washington, D.C., to Camden, New Jersey.

1876   Publishes "Centennial Edition" of *Leaves* in two volumes, one a reissue of the 1871 *Leaves* and the other entitled *Two Rivulets.* About this time begins rest and recuperation visits to the Stafford Farm on Timber Creek. English admirer Anne Gilchrist arrives in Philadelphia and begins long friendship with Whitman.

1879–1880 Travels West to Rockies; visits the alienist Dr. R. M. Bucke in Canada.

1881–1882 Publishes sixth edition of *Leaves,* dated 1881–82, in Boston, where it is banned when the Society for the Suppression of Vice finds the book immoral; publication transferred to Philadelphia.

1882 Publishes *Specimen Days & Collect.*

1883 Dr. R. M. Bucke publishes *Walt Whitman,* biography on which Whitman collaborates.

1884 Buys house on Mickle Street, Camden, New Jersey, where he will remain until his death.

1888 Paralysis increases; publishes *November Boughs.* Horace Traubel begins to record his visits.

1889 Publishes a volume combining the 1881 edition of *Leaves* with the 1882 *Specimen Days* and the 1888 *November Boughs.*

1891–1892 Publishes *Good-Bye My Fancy.* Issues the "authorized" *Leaves of Grass,* sometimes called the "deathbed edition"; the text is that of the sixth edition (1881–82) bound with the "Sands at Seventy" from the 1888 *November Boughs* and "Good-Bye My Fancy" from the 1891 pamphlet of that title (these clusters are called "Annexes").

1892 Dies 26 March; buried in tomb prepared in Harleigh Cemetery, Camden, New Jersey.

Chapter One
The Masks of Whitman

Walt Whitman wrote one book—*Leaves of Grass.* But he took a lifetime to write it, and he saw his one book through many shapes. Like a parent (he was unmarried and childless), he guided his poetic offspring through an uncertain, hesitant childhood, a lusty young manhood, and a serene old age. As biographers have found, it is difficult to write the life of Whitman without writing instead the life and times of his book. For Whitman was the kind of parent who lives his life through his child. In a very real sense, Whitman participated through his book in experiences he himself could only dream about; and he achieved the fulfillments of a richly involved and fully committed life only through his vital and pulsing offspring.

Near the end of his life, when Whitman sat down to compute the score in "A Backward Glance O'er Travel'd Roads," he confessed his conscious attempt to insert himself in his book. He wanted, he said, "to articulate and faithfully express in literary or poetic form, and un-compromisingly, my own physical, emotional, moral, intellectual, and aesthetic Personality, in the midst of, and tallying, the momentous spirit and facts of its immediate days, and of current America—and to exploit that Personality, identified with place and date, in a far more candid and comprehensive sense than any hitherto poem or book" (444).[1] This epic ambition, a kind of reverse cannibalism in which a book was to devour a man, dominated Whitman from the beginning. In his farewell poem for *Leaves of Grass,* he assumed his success: "Camerado, this is no book / Who touches this touches a man" (349).

But as Whitman said in "A Backward Glance," his book was meant to capture the Personality engaged in—or "tallying"—the "momentous spirit and facts of its immediate days." Whitman's days were, indeed, days of momentous spirit for him and for America. He was born in 1819 into a rural country raw and rude and bumbling from its recent birth. He witnessed the young blustery braggart blunder his way into a seemingly romantic and adventurous war that turned out to be a holocaust serving as the supreme test for the initiation into maturity of the young nation. And he was present for the lusty and materialistic consolidation, the plundering and the building, that signaled the change to an industrial and urban society, self-assured and settled.

In short, Whitman lived through the nation's heroic age, at a time when people had to be (or seemed to be) a little more than life-size to accomplish all the deeds they undertook. When he came on the scene, he found a country (like himself) in search of an identity. By the time he departed, not only he but his country had established, for better or worse, their personalities. Because Whitman and America conducted simultaneously that sobering search for a self, because they set off together in quest of their souls, there is an intimacy between the two in his book that no subsequent work can ever approach. *Leaves of Grass* must, for this reason, be recognized ultimately as America's great archetypal poem—as the national epic.

As though in anticipation of scholars and critics who would probe deeply into his private affairs, Whitman placed a warning at the beginning of *Leaves of Grass*:

> When I read the book, the biography famous,
> And is this then (said I) what the author calls a man's life?
> And so will someone when I am dead and gone write my life?
> (As if any man really knew aught of my life,
> Why even I myself I often think know little or nothing of my real life,
> Only a few hints, a few diffused clews and indirections
> I seek for my own use to trace out here.)
>
> (10)

A little reflection will confirm Whitman's point: no man's life was ever captured and placed between the covers of a book. The real substance of life, the spiritual involvements and the emotional undercurrents, the inner visions and the intimate prophecies—these deepest elements of a man's life must of necessity from their very nature escape recording. The biographer must deal with the outward show and the public view, or with whatever glimpses of these lesser elements the few surviving fragments of records permit.

As Whitman suggests, the reader who would know his life must read his book, and even there he will find only a "few diffused faint clews." As an introduction to Whitman, however, it will be useful to view a series of snapshots of him at various stages of his life. Admittedly, these will be exterior views, but they may offer hints (or indirections) as to his inner nature. As we view Whitman in his successive phases, we may jump to the conclusion that he was playing a series of roles, that he was a poseur and something of a phony.[2] But surely such a conclusion is hasty and superficial. Like any individual of depth and complexity, Whitman was continuously curious about who he was. If he seems at times to have overdramatized himself in certain roles, we should not accuse him of insincerity but of a lusty enthusiasm, a hearty relish for life lived at all times to its fullest intensity.

There Was a Child Went Forth

Whitman was born 31 May 1819, in West Hills, Long Island. His mother, Louisa Van Velsor, and his father, Walter, were semiliterate parents of nine children, of whom two proved to be imbeciles. The father earned a meager living, first at farming, than at laboring, building, and carpentry. The mother was closer to her son Walt. Her interest in Quakerism was the only religious inheritance the family passed on to the future poet. As he later came to idealize his mother, so he also came to romanticize his "Quaker" childhood. His use of "thee" and "thou" in his poetry, his reference to the months by their sequential number ("ninth month" for September), and his instinctive adoption of the doctrine of the inner light—all of these Walt could trace to his Quaker background.

In a family of such low literacy, no reliable accounts of Whitman's youth survive. When all of the external clues are put together, they still do not yield as persuasive a picture of the poet's childhood as that he himself painted in a few brief strokes in his poem "There Was a Child Went Forth." In relating what the child looked upon that "became part of him," the remembering poet catalogs the lilacs, the grass, the "sow's pink-faint litter"; the winter-grain sprouts, the apple trees, and the wood-berries; the "men and women crowding fast in the streets," the "huge crossing at the ferries," the schooner; the "hurrying tumbling waves," and "horizon's edge," the "fragrance of salt marsh and shore mud."

This jumble and mixture of country and city scenes, this fusion of vision of nature and man, must be near the truth, for the poet in childhood lived in alternation between the farm on Long Island and the streets of Brooklyn. Both the world of nature and the world of man

impinged forcefully on the young boy's imagination, and the mature
poet denied neither but exultingly embraced both.

In his poem of the child going forth, Whitman gives us a glimpse
of the domestic scene of his youth that tells much about the relationships in his household:

> The mother at home quietly placing the dishes on
> the supper-table,
> The mother with mild words, clean her cap and gown,
> a wholesome odor falling off her person and clothes
> as she walks by,
> The father, strong, self-sufficient, manly, mean,
> anger'd, unjust,
> The blow, the quick loud word, the tight bargain,
> the crafty lure,
> The family usages, the language, the company, the furniture,
> the yearning and swelling heart,
> Affection that will not be gainsay'd, the sense of what is
> real, the thought if after all it should prove unreal,
> The doubts of day-time and the doubts of
> night-time . . .
>
> (258–59)

The portraits of mother and father have the ring of truth, especially in
the young boy's involved view of them. The trailing off of the passage
from the concrete scene to metaphysical speculation, to thoughts about
the nature of reality—this surely must have been frequently the case
with the extraordinarily bright boy who some thought a lazy and
dreamy youth.

It is just possible that the youth's dreaminess, his restlessness spring-
ing from his daytime and nighttime doubts, made it difficult for him
to hold a position for any length of time. He left school at the age of
eleven and worked at a variety of jobs—as an office-boy, as a printer's
devil, as a printer, as a rural schoolteacher. Clearly he was unqualified
for schoolteaching not only because of the meagerness of his own aca-
demic background but also because of his dreamy and speculative temperament. For a period of some three years from the ages of about
seventeen to twenty—as he was emerging into young manhood—
Whitman drifted from rural school to rural school. He must soon
have come to the realization that he had not found his destined
labor.

Journalist and Dandy

It was natural that Whitman, with his genius and metaphysical in-
clinations, should have drifted into journalism, a profession that could
make some demands on his native endowments. As in schoolteaching,
he did not remain long in any one position. From the age of twenty to
thirty-six ʼwhen *Leaves of Grass* was born), and even beyond, Whitman
worked on various newspapers in and out of Brooklyn, including the
Long Islander, the New York *Aurora,* and the Brooklyn *Evening Star.*

At the age of twenty-seven, he became editor of the Brooklyn *Daily
Eagle,* a position of considerable consequence for such a young man.
His tenure did not last beyond two years, however, because of his pol-
itics. He was a Democrat and the paper was a Democratic organ, but
Whitman was a supporter of the Free-Soil party, which was opposed
to the extension of slavery to the new states coming into the Union.

Whitman's newspaper writings have all been resurrected and published, including his journalistic novel, *Franklin Evans; or, The Inebriate: A Tale of the Times* (1842), which was inept as a temperance plea
and worthless as fiction. These writings are of great bulk, filling many
volumes the size of Whitman's later work and masterpiece, *Leaves of
Grass.* But there is hardly a line in them (and there are some conventional poems scattered throughout) to match any of the great lines
tumbled forth in such heaps in the master work. In browsing through
these newspaper pieces, the reader can hardly escape the mystery at the
heart of Whitman—how did such an ordinary journalist transform
himself in midcareer, and without practice or warning, into America's
genius and epic poet?

A writer and editor—Whitman had by his own hands created himself in the proper image for these roles. If it is puzzling, in the light
of his later achievement, to know why his journalistic pieces were not
better than they were, it is just as puzzling, in the light of the meagerness of his formal preparation, to discover why they were as good
as they turned out to be. But Whitman is full of mysteries, of which
these are probably the least; it is perhaps ever thus with genius.

During his period as editor, Whitman was living the full life of the
city man—son of Manhattan. A rare photograph that survives from
this time shows him neatly bearded, his hat at a rakish angle, a cane
jauntily held in his hands, his face expressing the sophisticated self-
assurance of a man-about-town. Inevitably the photograph recalls
Whitman's claim in "Starting from Paumanok"—"No dainty dolce

affettuoso I." There is enough of the air of a "dainty dolce affettuoso" about the photograph to suggest that Whitman's later denial was the determined casting aside of a role once taken.

The polyglot Italian—*dolce* for sweet, *affettuoso* for one affected or pretending—would fit the period, for one of Whitman's greatest passions was the opera, an art form that the Italians claimed as their own. He was a veteran opera-goer, and the magnificent music and high melodrama made indelible impressions on his imagination, impressions that were to help shape the poetry of his masterpiece. At one point in "Song of Myself" he says:

> I hear the train'd soprano (what work with hers is this?)
> The orchestra whirls me wider than Uranus flies,
> It wrenches such ardors from me I did not know
>   I possess'd them,
>
>   (44)

This confession of passionate involvement with the music of opera can probably be taken literally, especially if we are to judge by the impact of the art form on *Leaves of Grass*. Such a great poem as "Out of the Cradle Endlessly Rocking," with its "arias" and its "recitatives" (operatic terms which Whitman himself used), reveals that Whitman's free-verse forms owe much to opera—its structure, its music, and the flow of the lines across the pages of the libretto.[3]

Vagabond on the Open Road

> Afoot and light-hearted I take to the open road,
> Healthy, free, the world before me,
> The long brown path before me leading wherever
>   I choose.
>
>   (108)

With these words Whitman steps forth from the pages of *Leaves of Grass* as the vagabond setting out to wander the high roads of the earth—"done with indoor complaints, libraries, querulous criticisms." No longer the "dainty dolce affettuoso," he proclaims: "Bearded, sunburnt, gray-neck'd, forbidding, I have arrived, / To be wrestled with as I pass for the solid prizes of the universe" (22). This sunburnt, athletic wrestler, this vagabond poet and wandering minstrel (whose slouching, open-shirted picture appeared in the 1855 *Leaves*) is difficult to discover outside the covers of *Leaves of Grass*—difficult, that is, until 1848, when Whitman for the first time escaped the confines of a life lived for some twenty-eight years within a small, geographical area on Long Island.

In accepting a job on a newspaper in New Orleans, Whitman made it possible for himself for the first time to see the vast stretches and varied landscapes of America that he was later to celebrate with such vigor in his songs, as in

> I hear America singing, the varied carols I hear,
> Those of mechanics, each one singing his as it should be
> blithe and strong,
> The carpenter singing his as he measures his plank or beam,
> (12)

Whitman had to be something of a vagabond traveling the open roads and coursing rivers of America just to get to New Orleans in 1848. He set out with his brother Jeff in February, traveling by rail to Baltimore and Cumberland, by coach over the mountains through the Cumberland Gap, by boat down the Ohio and, from Cairo, Illinois, on down the great muddy Mississippi to the semi-French port city of Louisiana. He returned by way of the Great Lakes and Canada, with a look at Niagara Falls before taking a boat down the Hudson to Brooklyn.

Although Whitman was gone only about four months as calendars count time, his imagination was permanently liberated from the provincialism of his small corner of the world. His vision of America was enlarged to embrace its vast prairies, its treacherous and rapid rivers, its raw frontiers and its refined metropolises—and its melting pot of a citizenry in the lively and bubbling processes of merging and fusing. What he did not see of the lands that lay west of the brown continental river he was now prepared to conceive through the restless, churning energy of his vigorous imagination.

It was once thought that Whitman experienced some intense love affair or passionate friendship in New Orleans that became the seed that was to flower forth after seven years of gestation as *Leaves of Grass*.[4] One of the poems of comradeship in the "Calamus" section of the book lends support to the idea:

I saw in Louisiana a live-oak growing,
All alone stood it and the moss hung down from the branches,
Without any companion it grew there uttering joyous leaves
      of dark green,
And its look, rude, unbending, lusty made me think of myself,
But I wonder'd how it could utter joyous leaves standing alone
      there without its friend near, for I knew I could not.

                                                                  (93)

Though the lone Louisiana tree seems clearly to symbolize a close
friend—perhaps a fellow writer "uttering joyous leaves"—there is no
need to build such slight evidence into some kind of fundamental personal attachment that seared Whitman's soul. Whitman's Creole romance was with America herself. Her mammoth embrace freed his
imagination from all its bonds and restrictions; it soared out in all its
glorious, unencumbered, and naked freedom to view from aloft and
afar the paths that lay behind, the roads that pointed ahead. Whitman
had only one lasting love affair, and that was with America—the
America of his dream: it was the affair that bestowed upon him the
ecstasy of his vision; and the only progeny was the solitary but magnificent creation—*Leaves of Grass*.

Carpenter-Christ

Upon his return to Brooklyn in June 1848, Whitman turned to
journalism once again, but his political beliefs against the extension of
slavery caused difficulty, and he finally turned to his father's trade—
carpentry. Just how extensively Whitman worked with his hands is
open to question. But it seems clear enough that he did know carpentry
intimately (its terms show up in the poetry—"plumb in the uprights,
well entretied, braced in the beams" [26]) and that he was engaged in
the building trade much as his father before him.

A photograph taken just before the appearance of the first edition of
Leaves catches the dreamy-eyed poet in just the right light to suggest
a halo. And there is an expression of infinite and endless sympathy
suffusing the face and extending out to the viewer. It would not take
much retouching, as Whitman must have known, to transfigure the
photograph into a portrait of Christ. The shirt open at the neck, with
the darker undergarment visible—all suggest the divine worker, the
humble carpenter filled with a boundless love for mankind.

Audacious as it may seem, Whitman was later to cast himself in the role of Christ. In one short poem that got him into difficulties with the censors, "To a Common Prostitute," he said:

> Not till the sun excludes you do I exclude you,
> Not till the waters refuse to glisten for you and the leaves
>   to rustle for you, do my words refuse to glisten
>   and rustle for you.
>
> My girl I appoint with you an appointment, and I charge you
>   that you make preparation to be worthy to meet me,
> And I charge you that you be patient and perfect till
>   I come.
>
> (273)

The public moralists did not see that the speaker of the poem was the poet filling the role of Christ and taking unto himself as did the Savior even the prostitute.

In a key passage of his long poem "Song of Myself," Whitman again identifies himself with Christ:

> That I could forget the mockers and insults!
> That I could forget the trickling tears and the blows of the
>   bludgeons and hammers!
> That I could look with a separate look on my own crucifixion
>   and bloody crowning!
>
> . . . .
>
> The grave of rock multiplies what has been confided to it,
>   or to any graves,
> Corpses rise, gashes heal, fastenings roll from me.
>
> I troop forth replenish'd with supreme power, one of an
>   average unending procession,
>
> (56)

In this, as in so many passages in *Leaves of Grass,* Whitman seems to be playing a double role; he assumes the likeness of Christ, and he seems also to be everyman become Christ ("one of an average"). Throughout a long portion of "Song of Myself," he flies swiftly about the earth, mystically sharing his supreme spiritual power with the hurt and the troubled, the sick and the dying.

Whitman did not have delusions of grandeur. His assumption of the role of Christ in his book was for a specific poetic purpose—one not unlike the identification of Melville's Billy Budd with Christ, or of Steinbeck's Jim Casy, or of Faulkner's Joe Christmas. W. D. O'Connor, one of Whitman's early literary friends, was so impressed by Whitman in this role that he wrote *The Carpenter* (1868), a thinly disguised portrayal of Whitman as the Christ. But however much Whitman cultivated the role of Christ, in public pose or in poetic mask, he did not attempt to found a religion or develop a cult. He said in "Song of Myself": "No friend of mine takes his ease in my chair, / I have no chair, no church, no philosophy" (64). Whitman openly discouraged his enthusiastic followers, those who later became known as the "hot little prophets,"[5] from hailing him as a deity and using his *Leaves* as a modern Bible.

An American Bard at Last

According to legend, Whitman published the 1855 edition of *Leaves of Grass* on the Fourth of July. He was thirty-six years old. In every sense, the publication was an instance of self-reliance and independence. Whitman, an old hand with type, set up some of the pages himself, and he was intimately involved in the book's distribution. The edition of a thousand did not sell well, nor was there a deluge of reviews. To remedy this situation, the poet sent many copies of his book to literary notables, and also wrote three unsigned reviews himself.

These reviews (included in *In Re Walt Whitman,* 1893) turn out to be some of the most valuable biographical data in existence, for they not only give Whitman's evaluation of his own work, but they provide a self-portrait at this most crucial turning point in Whitman's life— when he put aside forever the ordinary pursuits of a livelihood and dedicated himself to poetry. The self-image cannot, of course, be taken at face value. Whitman wrote the reviews for the public. But though they might not present Whitman as he actually was, they certainly do present him as he thought he appeared in his poetry: they reveal Whitman exclaiming at his own poetic mask.

One of the reviews opens: "An American bard at last! One of the roughs, large, proud, affectionate, eating, drinking, and breeding, his costume manly and free, his face sunburnt and bearded, his postures strong and erect, his voice bringing hope and prophecy to the generous races of young and old."[6] America had long been looking for a true poet. Some thought Bryant had become America's poet through his use of native flowers and birds in his poetry. Others thought that Longfellow had made himself the long-sought poet by his use of native lore and legends in such poems as "Hiawatha," also first published in 1855. But these poets and others had spoken with the cultivated accents, the refined tones, of the tradition of British poetry.

Who can deny that Whitman's pose did the trick? His accents were primitive, his tones crude—and he boasted about it. He was not a poet, but a bard, a chanter of chants, a singer of songs. He was one of the common people, one of the outdoor roughs, rude and unlettered, healthy and athletic: "Self-reliant, with haughty eyes, assuming to himself all the attributes of his country, steps Walt Whitman into literature, talking like a man unaware that there was ever hitherto such a production as a book, or such a being as a writer."[7] In short, Whitman pointed to himself as the bardic prophet, the primitive seer, the American frontiersman democratically sharing his elemental wisdom. In his 1855 Preface to *Leaves of Grass,* Whitman defined the poet's function as seer: "The greatest poet hardly knows pettiness or triviality. If he breathes into anything that was before thought small it dilates with the grandeur and life of the universe. He is a seer" (415). The poet becomes seer by the profundity of his gaze not into the future but into the present, into things as they are, into the deepest significance of a blade of grass or a grain of sand.

American, democrat, bard, and prophet—Whitman thus saw himself reflected in his *Leaves.* The extent of the pose can be measured by the length of Whitman's journalistic apprenticeship—some fifteen years, a long time around books to remain unread, a long time around writing not to meet writers. But the discrepancy between the pose and the reality is superficial and beside the point. Whitman was not playacting. He had in reality made himself over, re-created himself, and he became symbolically what he said he was. There was powerful, bold, imaginative validity in his mask—and that is what counts in poetry.

In one of his reviews, Whitman described his physical self in vivid detail: "Of pure American breed, large and lusty—age thirty-six years, (1855,)—never once using medicine—never dressed in black, always dressed freely and clean in strong clothes—neck open, shirt collar flat and broad, countenance tawny transparent red, beard well-mottled with white, hair like hay after it has been mowed in the field and lies tossed and streaked—his physiology corroborating a rugged phrenology. . . .[8] Clearly Whitman had the faculty of being able to stand aside and see himself as he appeared, or wanted to appear, to others; or, as he put it in "Song of Myself": "Both in and out of the game and watching and wondering at it" (27). The game was life, and in it he maintained his pose.

His "rugged phrenology" is of more than passing interest. Phrenology was the psychology or psychiatry of Whitman's day, and many people (Poe, for example) believed in it. The "science" consisted of reading the bumps on the head, the sizes of the bumps offering clues to the various traits of personality determined by the contours of the brain beneath. In a long footnote to his review, Whitman printed his own chart of bumps as constructed by a phrenologist: "Size of head large, 23 inches. Leading traits appear to be Friendship, Sympathy, Sublimity, and Self-Esteem, and markedly among its combinations the dangerous faults of Indolence, a tendency to the pleasures of Voluptuousness and Alimentiveness, and a certain reckless swing of animal will."[9]

The numbers "1" to "7" were assigned to the various categories to indicate degree of development. The categories were given terms which, much like those of a pseudoscience today, were semimysterious and jargonistic: Philoprogenitiveness, Alimentiveness, Inhabitiveness, Amativeness, Adhesiveness. These last two terms were especially important to Whitman; he used them as summary terms for two of his important themes: Amativeness for man-woman love, as in his "Children of Adam" poems; Adhesiveness for man-man love, or comradeship, as in his "Calamus" poems.[10]

Bohemian

The small sale of the 1855 edition of *Leaves of Grass* did not discourage Whitman from publishing a new edition, with a great many new poems, in 1856. This second edition was hurried through the press to serve in part as a reply to a letter that Ralph Waldo Emerson had written, 21 July 1855, extolling the original edition. Emerson's letter was extravagant, and Whitman was elated—so elated that he used a phrase from Emerson's letter, together with Emerson's name, on the spine of the new edition—"I greet you at the beginning of a great career."

The large number of new poems in the second edition must have kept Whitman busy as a poet the full year preceding its appearance.

And the still larger number of new poems that were printed in the third edition, in 1860, suggest that this period, 1855–60, was Whitman's most productive one, a time of concentrated creativity when Whitman was in every sense of the word a practicing poet. No longer a journalist, no longer a carpenter, Whitman was during this period in the process of establishing his identity, not only for the public and posterity, but also for himself. He was discovering at last just who he was: "I celebrate myself, and sing myself, / And what I assume you shall assume, / For every atom belonging to me as good belongs to you" (25).

As poet and artist, it is understandable that he would find his true milieu not in the literary gentility of Boston but in the relaxed bohemianism of New York. Emerson's private recognition was never accorded in public, and such respectable fireside poets as Holmes and Longfellow could not embrace such vulgarity; Whittier was said to have thrown his copy of the 1855 *Leaves* into the fire. Besides Emerson, only Thoreau seemed to recognize the genius of the Brooklyn bard, and sought him out to pay his respects.

Whitman gravitated by both necessity and inclination to the society of bohemian New York. He had no taste for the formal, the stuffy, the important, and the celebrated. He described himself (in one of his reviews): "never on platforms amid the crowds of clergymen, or professors, or aldermen, or congressmen—rather down in the bay with pilots in their pilot-boat—or off on a cruise with fishers in a fishing-smack—or riding on a Broadway omnibus, side by side with the driver—or with a band of loungers over the open grounds of the country—fond of New York and Brooklyn—fond of the life of the great ferries."[11] There is no reason to doubt the sincerity of Whitman's sentiments. There is ample evidence that he not only enjoyed the kind of companionship he described but prized it above any cultivation of the great.

For literary comradeship, Whitman frequented a Broadway bohemian beer parlor and restaurant known as Pfaff's—a hangout for the unconventional, the daring, the clever, and the witty. At Pfaff's could be found Henry Clapp, editor of the advanced *Saturday Press,* where Whitman first published "Out of the Cradle Endlessly Rocking" (as "A Child's Reminiscence"). Whitman's friend and the "Queen of Bohemia," Ada Clare, had gone to Paris to have her illegitimate child. Others who turned up were Thomas Bailey Aldrich, E. C. Stedman, and R. E. Stoddard.

As a young man, William Dean Howells, choosing between Boston and New York as a place to establish himself, had sought Whitman out at Pfaff's. He left a vivid portrait of Whitman in bohemia: "he leaned back in his chair, and reached out his great hand to me, as if he were going to give it me for good and all. He had a fine head, with a cloud of Jovian hair upon it, and a branching beard and mustache, and gentle eyes that looked most kindly into mine, and seemed to wish the liking which I instantly gave him, though we hardly passed a word, and our acquaintance was summed up in that glance and the grasp of his mighty fist upon my hand."[12] However moved Howells was by the meeting, his final choice in his dilemma was respectable Boston over bohemian New York.

Whitman was no doubt attracted to bohemian society by his own innate taste for close companionship and his belief in sexual frankness and honesty. And he no doubt found in this social intercourse reinforcement for the elements already existent in his own nature. Whatever the case, the 1860 edition of *Leaves of Grass* was the most daring of the early editions, bringing together in concentrated clusters the sex poems and the comradeship poems. It was a kind of bohemian defiance that enabled Whitman to set out in his poetry to break the old restraints and conventions:

> From pent-up aching rivers,
> From that of myself without which I were nothing,
> From what I am determin'd to make illustrious, even if I
>   stand sole among men,
> From my own voice resonant, singing the phallus,
> Singing the song of procreation,
> Singing the need of superb children and therein superb
>   grown people,
> Singing the muscular urge and the blending,
>   (69)

If Whitman was willing to "stand sole among men" in order to sing the "song of procreation," he was no less willing to defy society in order to "celebrate the need of comrades":

> From all the standards hitherto publish'd, from the pleasures,
>   profits, conformities,
> Which too long I was offering to feed my soul,

> Clear to me now standards not yet publish'd, clear to me that
> my soul,
> That the soul of the man I speak for rejoices in comrades,
>
> (84)

Many essayists before Whitman, including Emerson and Montaigne, had written pairs of essays treating the complementary subjects of love and friendship. Whitman took this tradition and deepened it, probing to the naked soul of the relationships as no one before him had done. In his bohemian daring he seemed not only to brush aside the Victorian conformity and convention of his time, but also to have anticipated the modern sexual psychology of Freud.

Wound-Dresser

> (Arous'd and angry, I'd thought to beat the alarum,
> and urge relentless war,
> But soon my fingers fail'd me, my face droop'd and I
> resign'd myself,
> To sit by the wounded and soothe them, or silently watch
> the dead;)
>
> (221)

Whitman might well have lived out his life genially and meaninglessly in New York's bohemia had not some great overriding cause appeared on the horizon. Although he had early in his journalistic career taken a passionate interest in politics, and had supported the Free-Soil party, his political interests later flagged as his artistic involvements intensified. He did not anticipate the Civil War; but, when the news of the firing on Fort Sumter arrived in New York, making clear that a great national struggle was underway, Whitman was aroused from his minor personal interests to renewed creative vigor and vision. Forty-one years old at the outbreak of the war, he was beyond the age of enlistment and, besides, he had the responsibility of caring for his mother (his father had died in 1855).

But Whitman was destined for involvement in the strife and bloodshed. His brother George enlisted immediately, rose by distinguishing himself in action to the rank of first lieutenant, and in late 1862 was wounded near Fredericksburg, Virginia. The appearance of his name

in a list of wounded in a New York paper was the signal that Whitman
had been waiting for. He set off immediately for Virginia to find his
brother. As it turned out, George's wound was superficial; but Walt's
trip wrought profound changes in his life.

On his way to Virginia he had passed through Washington, D. C.,
and had observed there the pain and agony of great numbers of
wounded that overflowed the hospitals into the public buildings.
There were inadequate facilities, doctors, nurses, help of any kind. The
image of the great mass of suffering soldiers preyed on Whitman's
mind: he set himself up as a kind of one-man Red Cross (in the days
before that organization existed). After taking a minor position with
the government that required only a few hours of his time each day,
he circulated through the hospitals, bringing to the wounded a few
material comforts (writing paper, magazines) but offering much
more—himself with all his fellow feeling and deep human sympathies:

> Returning, resuming, I thread my way through the hospitals,
> The hurt and wounded I pacify with soothing hand,
> I sit by the restless all the dark night, some are so young,
> Some suffer so much, I recall the experience sweet and sad,
> (Many a soldier's loving arms about this neck have cross'd
>   and rested,
> Many a soldier's kiss dwells on these bearded lips.)
>
> (222)

The Civil War was a turning point not only in Whitman's life but
in the nation's. Whitman's glimpses of the battlefields in his search for
his brother, together with his intimate knowledge of the hospitals
filled with the wounded of both the Blue and the Gray, impressed
themselves vividly on his imagination. Out of his deep emotional involvement he found material for new poems. Heretofore Whitman had
discovered his material in his own personality, in the self he had celebrated so defiantly and the ego he had flung out with pride. The war
provided exactly the kinds of experiences needed to draw Whitman's
image-making faculty out of its own narcissistic fascination with itself;
but, at the same time, had he not spent the long beginning of his life
in contemplation of his own kaleidoscopic soul, he probably would not
have found the depths from which to summon the overflowing sympathy that he offered to the soldiers:

'Twas well, O soul—'twas a good preparation you gave me,
Now we advance our latent and ampler hunger to fill,
Now we go forth to receive what the earth and the sea
    never gave us,
Not through the mighty woods we go, but through the
mightier cities,
Something for us is pouring now more than Niagara pouring,
Torrents of men, (sources and rills of the Northwest are you
    indeed inexhaustible?)

(209)

His imagination stirred from its lethargy and fired with a new purpose and enthusiasm, Whitman poured out new poems—not in the
volume in which they came in the earlier period, but still in abun·
dance. There were enough to make a small book by themselves, published in 1865 as *Drum-Taps*. Shortly after its appearance, President
Abraham Lincoln was assassinated, and again Whitman felt the agonizing involvement in events remote from himself that produced great
poetry. "O Captain! My Captain!" was the kind of public tribute that
Longfellow might have written. But "When Lilacs Last in the Dooryard Bloom'd" was a personal chant welling out of emotional depths
that only Whitman could have written. Lincoln and Whitman had
never met, but legend tells that the president had read and admired
Leaves of Grass, and certain it is that Whitman had looked upon and
admired Lincoln as he passed in his carriage through the streets of
Washington.[13] Whitman's Lincoln poems were soon added as an annex
to the *Drum-Taps* volume.

If his relationship with Lincoln was the kind of comradeship that
Whitman had celebrated in his poetry, but on an idealized and imaginative plane, his relationship with Peter Doyle, a youthful, illiterate
horse-car conductor and ex-Confederate Army soldier whom he met
one night in Washington, was for Whitman the real thing, though no
doubt idealized too. Whitman had always drawn many of his closest
friends from the nonliterary, even the illiterate class—from among
New York's bus drivers and ferry-boat crews. But only of his comradeship with Doyle does a record exist, in the form of a series of letters
from Whitman to Doyle (published after Whitman's death as *Calamus*);
these express the deep affection, in the main paternalistic, that the
older poet felt for the youth.[14]

During his days in Washington, Whitman had always held some

tenuous position with the government. In 1865 he was released from his job in the Department of the Interior by Secretary James Harlan, who gave economy as the reason for the unexpected act. But it soon became clear that Harlan had come across Whitman's marked-up copy of *Leaves of Grass* in his desk. In this copy Whitman had underscored lines and poems for transference or deletion in a new edition, and many of these were sexual and procreative passages. Whitman was really fired for his "obscene" poetry.

The outcome of the incident helped rather than harmed Whitman and his reputation. Friends got him an immediate transfer to the Attorney General's office and he suffered no loss of pay. But more important, two of his closest comrades published defenses of him. W. D. O'Connor, a novelist who had sought out Whitman as a friend in Washington, wrote a fiery, impassioned defense in *The Good Gray Poet* (1866); in it he deified Whitman by placing him alongside Buddha and Christ and ranked his poetry with Homer's and Shakespeare's. John Burroughs, the naturalist in whose home Whitman was a frequent visitor, followed O'Connor with a more balanced book, *Notes on Walt Whitman as Poet and Person* (1867). These two works did much more than simply defend Whitman from the charge of obscenity: they emphasized his innocence and saintliness of character and they defined his themes and explained his forms to the public. For the first time Whitman's reputation was promoted by informed, articulate voices that would be heard. In the light of all the previous neglect, the exaggeration of these early estimates by the "hot little prophets" was surely excusable.

A Batter'd, Wreck'd Old Man

Clearly 1861, with the coming of the Civil War, marked a turning point for Whitman: he shed his past and began a new career with new poetry and new themes. In a like way, 1873 brought Whitman private disasters which took their toll and necessitated change. In this year he entered still another phase of his life, both personal and creative. Early in 1873, at the age of fifty-four, Whitman suffered a paralytic stroke that left him incapacitated and drained of energy. To a poet who had made of the healthy, potent body one of the primary virtues, this disabling illness was a personal catastrophe.

Still another blow fell in May 1873, when Whitman's mother died. Whitman had opened one of his poems ("Starting from Paumanok"):

"Starting from fish-shape Paumanok where I was born, / Well-begotten, and rais'd by a perfect mother" (15). He had never concealed his partiality for his mother, and in his absences from home he had kept up a correspondence that revealed a strong attachment. Her death was felt as a terrible loss, leaving him more alone and isolated than ever. Declining in energy and feeling intense loneliness, Whitman was passing through the greatest depression of his life—a depression that required major adjustment in his ultimate removal from Washington and a return to the area of his origin. Finally he settled in Camden, New Jersey, to watch out the remaining years of his life.

As before in his career, Whitman found in his emotional plight the materials with which his imagination could construct poems. One of the poems from this period, "Prayer of Columbus," was a symbolic embodiment of Whitman's own situation:

> A batter'd, wreck'd old man,
> Thrown on this savage shore, far, far from home,
> Pent by the sea and dark rebellious brows, twelve
>   dreary months,
> Sore, stiff with many toils, sicken'd and nigh to death,
> I take my way along the island's edge,
> Venting a heavy heart.
>
>   (295)

Although the feelings clearly were the poet's in his time of agonizing trial, he was still able to project them in the soliloquy of Columbus, transfiguring them dramatically into one of his finest short poems.

Shortly after he took up residence in Camden, Whitman found the best treatment for his maladies on a friend's nearby secluded farm called Timber Creek. Here he spent a number of successive summers, relaxing in the midst of nature, sometimes nude in the sun. This treatment restored strength both to his weakened body and his wounded spirit. Finding no aspect of his life too little or insignificant to feed his imagination, Whitman recorded his times on Timber Creek in a series of journal entries later published in *Specimen Days* (1882). He wrote of a typical day (Sunday, 27 August 1877): "Another day quite free from mark'd prostration and pain. It seems indeed as if peace and nutriment from heaven subtly filter into me as I slowly hobble down these country lanes and across fields, in the good air—as I sit here in solitude with Nature—open, voiceless, mystic, far-removed, yet palpable, eloquent

Nature. I merge myself in the scene, in the perfect day. . . . Every
day, seclusion—every day at least two or three hours of freedom, bathing, no talk, no bonds, no dress, no books, *no manners.*"[15]

There is no record that Whitman ever proposed marriage to any
woman; there is on record a proposal of marriage made to him by a
woman. It is perhaps ironic that this proposal would materialize at a
time of his physical decline, for it was inspired in part by the earlier
poetic pictures of himself in glorious health. Anne Gilchrist was the
widow of William Blake's famous biographer, Alexander Gilchrist. She
had strong literary interests, which enabled her to conclude the work
on Blake that her husband left unfinished. She came across the English
edition of *Leaves of Grass* (which had been edited in 1867 by William
Michael Rossetti) and responded passionately to its personal tone and
intimate appeal. She began a correspondence with Whitman, writing
him what were in effect love letters, and she published an article on
his poetry.[16] Whitman's replies were polite but restrained; they did not
prevent her from coming to America in 1876 to set up housekeeping
in Philadelphia, close to Camden. There she and her children became
fast friends of the poet, and they helped to alleviate the loneliness of
his declining years. Though romance did not develop, there were mutual regard and respect valued by both the widow and the poet.

Bearded Sage

It would be misleading to suggest that Whitman lived out the remainder of his life a battered wreck. Although he never recovered the
full health of his prime, he did by dint of his powerful will nurse
himself back to a strength and vitality sufficient to avoid becoming an
invalid. During these last years, his reputation was growing; and that
popular image of the poet as a bearded sage, familiar to the school
walls of the nation, was becoming fixed. This image of Whitman as
an old man, as an ancient pious philosopher, has become so rigid that
many people are taken completely by surprise by the youth and vigor
and physical esprit of the major poems that crowd the pages of *Leaves
of Grass.*

As proof of some return to physical vigor, Whitman made an extended journey in 1879 to visit parts of the country in the far West
which, though he had embraced them in his poetry, he had never seen.
It was, of course, too late in his life to expect an impact like that of
the 1848 New Orleans journey which had awakened latent creative

powers. But Whitman's imagination was inspired anew by the raw, grotesque landscapes. He wrote in Platte Cañon, Colorado:

> Spirit that form'd this scene,
> These tumbled rock-piles grim and red,
> These reckless heaven-ambitious peaks,
> These gorges, turbulent-clear streams, this naked freshness,
> These formless wild arrays, for reasons of their own,
> I know thee, savage spirit—we have communed together,
> Mine too such wild arrays, for reasons of their own;
>
> (337)

In this wild abandon of western scene, Whitman found counterpart and confirmation of the wild, free spirit that formed his poetry. Though he looked upon the scene for the first time in his old age, he believed that he had long since communed with its living spirit in the early *Leaves of Grass.*

By far the most significant activity of Whitman during the closing years of his life was putting the final touches on his masterpiece. There were editions involving major additions, regroupings, and transferences in 1867 and 1871. The "Centennial Edition" of 1876 was in two volumes—one was a reissue of the 1871 *Leaves* and the other, *Two Rivulets,* contained miscellaneous prose and many poems grouped under the title "Passage to India"; it also had a preface which suggested that the poet was starting a new volume of primarily spiritual poems as a companion for his more physical *Leaves.* But by the time of the appearance of the sixth edition of *Leaves of Grass* in 1881, Whitman had abandoned any such plans and had placed all of his major poems in the master volume. Though there were new issues of *Leaves* in 1889 and 1891–92 (the so-called deathbed edition) in which the poet inserted "Annexes" containing poems of his last days, the 1881 edition contained the final structure of his book as he had painstakingly worked it out over a period of some twenty-five years.

It is ironic that this edition, the crowning achievement of his lifetime of poetic labor, was the one banned in Boston. The firm of Osgood and Company there had undertaken to publish the 1881 *Leaves*; but when Whitman withstood pressure to delete a number of poems and lines the publisher withdrew the book and turned the plates over to Whitman. Publication followed immediately in Philadelphia, as Whitman once again triumphed over his would-be censors.

Whitman published other books during these later years. His torturedly reasoned defense of American democracy, not as it is but as it could be, appeared in *Democratic Vistas* in 1871. A semiautobiographical volume, stuffed with reminiscences and diary notes and leftover jottings, appeared as *Specimen Days & Collect* in 1882–83. A volume of miscellaneous prose and poetry, *November Boughs,* containing "A Backward Glance O'er Travel'd Roads," appeared in 1888. But Whitman's main creative efforts went into the final shaping of his *Leaves* in its successive editions.

During these final days, too, there were friends and comrades. One of Whitman's close associates, a strong admirer, was Dr. Richard Maurice Bucke, a Canadian psychologist who wrote, with Whitman's collaboration, a biography of the poet in 1883. His long association with Whitman and his firm belief in the profundity of *Leaves of Grass* led him later to an arresting and original study of *Cosmic Consciousness* (1901) in which he ranked Whitman with the great religious and poetic mystics of all time. A younger man and disciple, Horace Traubel, became a kind of Boswell to Whitman in his old age, paying him extended visits and holding long conversations with him. He scrupulously recorded every detail. In 1906 he began publication of a series of large volumes under the title *With Walt Whitman in Camden,* containing verbatim all of his copious notes about his visits with the Good Gray Poet.

Whitman was not unprepared for his death. He had portrayed death as a "strong deliveress" in "When Lilacs Last in the Dooryard Bloom'd," and he had even dramatized his own dissolution at the end of "Song of Myself." The cry in the poem—"And as to you Death, and you bitter hug of mortality, it is idle to try to alarm me"—had been no empty boast. He had taken "death" as one of his major themes, and he had many years before his own confrontation written the farewell poem to conclude his book, "So Long!":

> I feel like one who has done work for the day to retire awhile,
> I receive now again of my many translations, from my
>   avataras ascending, while others doubtless await me,
> An unknown sphere more real than I dream'd, more direct,
>   darts awakening rays about me, *So long!*
> Remember my words, I may again return,
> I love you, I depart from materials,
> I am as one disembodied, triumphant, dead.
>
>   (350)

When he died from a complex of illnesses in 1892, at the age of seventy-two, he could take some satisfaction in a life fulfilled and completed. He had made his book, and he had left it to the world as he wanted it. Death was a natural part of the pose that he had dramatized in his poetry. Death rounded off the role that he had assigned to himself in life.

Chapter Two
Growth of the *Leaves*

Leaves of Grass grew, much of its own accord, like a seed that contains within itself from the very beginning all its potential of size and shape. Whitman tended the seed, carefully cultivated it, and tried at times to abandon it; but he always returned to it, sometimes to prune, sometimes to graft, always to encourage fulfillment of its destined design. In all there were some six lifetime editions of *Leaves*, plus three additional reprintings with new dates and bindings, over a period of thirty years; each of the editions represented a stage in its growth that sent forth its own individual fruit and seeds. Seldom in the history of art have we been so privileged with such an intimate view of the creation of a masterpiece.

The miracle of Whitman is that, at the age of thirty-six, without warning or notice, suggestion or hint, he brought forth a volume of poetry that would have graced the literature of any nation, and which, even had it stood unchanged, would have assured his fame as a poet. Whitman sent a copy of the 1855 edition to Ralph Waldo Emerson, who was then the ruling genius of American letters. It was in great part the *anonymity* of this impassioned poet that caused Emerson to rub his eyes—and to sit down and strike off in the glow of his immediate response a small letter that was to have the largest reverberations of any letter in American literature:

I am not blind to the worth of the wonderful gift of *Leaves of Grass*. I find it the most extraordinary piece of wit and wisdom that America has yet contributed. I am very happy in reading it, as great power makes us happy. It meets the demand I am making of what seemed the sterile and stingy nature, as if too much handiwork, or too much lymph in the temperament, were making our western wits fat and mean.

I give you joy of your free and brave thought. I have great joy in it. I find incomparable things said incomparably well, as they must be. I find the courage of treatment which so delights us, and which large perception only can inspire.

I greet you at the beginning of a great career, which yet must have had a long foreground somewhere, for such a start. I rubbed my eyes a little, to see if this sunbeam were no illusion; but the solid sense of the book is a sober certainty. It has the best merits, namely, of fortifying and encouraging.[1]

If Whitman had any doubts about his new dedication to poetry, Emerson's letter must have cleared them away. And even more than a century after it was written, Emerson's brief letter serves as a more perceptive commentary on Whitman's poetry than many an essay and book.

In suggesting that Whitman's career must have had "a long foreground somewhere," Emerson was crystallizing the critical problem that all Whitman students have at some time studied but left, finally, unresolved. The thirty-six years preceding publication of the first edition of *Leaves* have been scrutinized with minute care, but without discovery of the key to the mystery of Whitman's genius, without locating the signal experience that filled him to overflowing with the creative energy of his *Leaves*.

The problem is a difficult one because it cannot be solved by arranging a catalog of all the exterior events of Whitman's life and amplifying those that touch upon literature. Whitman wrote a great deal during these thirty-six years, for the newspapers and magazines, but little of what he wrote is readable, none of it memorable. He even wrote a number of poems:

> For vainly through this world below
> We seek affection. Nought but wo[e]
> Is with our earthly journey wove;
> And so the heart must look above,
>   Or die in dull despair.[2]

Such stale diction, such inept language-sense, and such conventional sentiment simply increase the mystery of Whitman's genius. Clearly it was running in currents deep beneath the surface of the poet, perhaps below the levels of consciousness, where for its long preparation it was seething and simmering and bubbling, biding its time and awaiting the proper moment to flood his conscious mind and to burst forth to public view like a pent-up river. In "Song of Myself" Whitman cried out: "Dazzling and tremendous how quick the sun-rise would kill me,/ If I could not now and always send sun-rise out of me" (43).

There remain for us some glimpses into this long, deep-down preparation in Whitman in the notebook jottings made during the late 1840s and early 1850s. In these personal, private notebooks, well kept from public view (and later quoted in the variorum readings in the 1902 *Complete Writings*), Whitman wrote the embryonic lines of some of the important passages of *Leaves of Grass*. It is astonishing to contemplate the poet leading a kind of creative double-life, carrying on his conventional writing in his journalistic jobs and ventures, and at the same time secretly testing on paper the unconventional, daring, profoundly felt passages of the as yet uncreated *Leaves*. Section 23 of "Song of Myself," devoted to extolling "positive science"—"I accept Reality and dare not question it,/Materialism first and last imbuing" (41)—appeared in its first form in the early notebooks:

> I am the poet of Reality,
> And I say the stars are not echoes,
> And I say that space is no apparition;
> But all the things seen or demonstrated are so;
> Witnesses and albic dawns of things equally great, yet not seen.
>
> I announce myself the Poet of Materials and exact demonstration;
> Say that Materials are just as eternal as growth, the semen of
>   God that swims the entire creation.[3]

These notebook lines give the impression of a visionary who, at the beginning, is just catching a few random glimpses of his vision, is yet uncertain that it will still come into full view, is unsure even himself of the meaning of what he sees and knows. As time passed, the lines multiplied and the passages swelled, until, by 1855, Whitman could hold it back no longer, and cried out: "Unclench your floodgates, you are too much for me" (46).

Undercurrents: Immense Have Been the Preparations for Me

Although Whitman's genius cannot be explained by marshalling all the elements that went into its making, its force and shape can be better understood by examining some of the influences that fed and inspired it. In his *Specimen Days*, Whitman went over this foreground of his life and remarked some of the situations and events of powerful impact. Although Whitman probably concealed (either consciously or unconsciously) as much as he revealed, his suggestions are worthy of note. In naming the three main sources of his character, he listed his "maternal nativity-stock" from the Netherlands, his "paternal English elements," and—the most tangible of all—"the combination of my Long Island birth-spot, sea-shores, childhood's scenes, absorptions, with teeming Brooklyn and New York. . . ."[4]

There is no reason to doubt that many of the most powerful lines of Whitman were written directly out of his experience—"Sea of stretch'd ground-swells, / Sea breathing broad and convulsive breaths" (40) or "The blab of the pave, tires of carts, sluff of bootsoles, talk of the promenaders" (30). Son of the sea and the city, absorbing both the seashore scenes and teeming Brooklyn, lover of both solitude and the crowds, Whitman found in his own earliest experiences the kind of paradox that resolved itself in his own soul. When he later placed at the opening of *Leaves* the lines "One's-self I sing, a simple separate person, / Yet utter the word Democratic, the word En-Masse" (5), he was setting forth the characteristic paradox that was to thread all through the *Leaves* and which grew naturally out of the earliest commitments of his childhood experiences.

When Whitman speaks of the sea's "convulsive breaths" and remarks on the "blab of the pave," he is noting a music of the natural world and of the city that cut deeply into his imagination. It is impossible to estimate how much his poetry was shaped by his early experiences, but it seems likely that they were dominant influences. There is a rough resemblance between the majestic roll of the waves out of the sea toward the shore and the sonorous roll of Whitman's long, flowing lines, one following close on the other. And there is a subterranean kinship between the hectic hustle and bustle of the city, with its mingling of people of all origins, kinds, and tongues, and the frantic skipping and skimming and hovering of Whitman's catalogs with their mingling of life of all descriptions and levels. Among romantic poets, Whitman appears unique in his absorption and celebration of both country and city. His poetry represents an imaginative fusion of the two, its very form resolving their opposition and reconciling their conflicting pulls.

But besides the sea and the pavement, the country and the city, there were other influences that shaped the poet. He wrote in *Specimen Days*: "while living in Brooklyn, (1835–50) I went regularly every week in the mild seasons down to Coney island, at that time a long, bare unfrequented shore, which I had all to myself, and where I loved, after bathing, to race up and down the hard sand, and declaim Homer or Shakspere to the surf and sea-gulls by the hour."[5] Homer and Shakespeare, surf and sea gulls—the suggestion of fusion is clear. Although Whitman's memory may be distorting slightly, there is no reason to doubt that he early identified himself with the great "archetypal" poetry of the past and recognized some obscure relationship between it and the primitive natural forces of the universe. His early knowledge of the world's classics formulated a scale with which he could measure his own ambition, while his imaginative fusing of them with surf and sea gulls served as a warning against literary imitation, against a too-literal emulation.

This early ideal persisted through Whitman's career, and in *Democratic Vistas* (1871) he was still calling for an American literature "vitalized by national, original archetypes" (486). In "A Backward Glance O'er Travel'd Roads" (1888), gossiping over his youth and his preparation for writing his *Leaves,* he instinctively thought in terms of the old Bibles and epics and classics. He recalled: "I used to go off, sometimes for a week at a stretch, down in the country, or to Long Island's seashores—there, in the presence of outdoor influences, I went over thoroughly the Old and New Testaments, and absorb'd (probably to better advantage for me than in any library or indoor room—it makes such difference *where* you read,) Shakspere [*sic*], Ossian, the best translated versions I could get of Homer, Eschylus, Sophocles, the old German Nibelungen, the ancient Hindoo poems, and one or two other masterpieces, Dante's among them. As it happen'd, I read the latter mostly in an old wood. The Iliad (Buckley's prose version) I read first thoroughly on the peninsula of Orient, northeast end of Long Island, in a shelter'd hollow of rocks and sand, with the sea on each side" (449–50).

The epic shape and prophetic drift of *Leaves of Grass* must owe much to Whitman's reading of the classics on Paumanok's beaches. It is difficult, for example, to calculate the debt his book owes to the Bible. In a late essay called "The Bible as Poetry," Whitman asked, "Could there be any more opportune suggestion, to the current popular writer and reader of verse, what the office of poet was in primeval times—and is yet capable of being, anew, adjusted entirely to the modern?"[6] He pointed to the Bible's "divine and primal poetic structure" as the element that would enable it to survive the religion it promulgates. Such respect sprang from his intimate and early knowledge of the Bible's simple rhythms and stately language, a knowledge that must have helped create the *Leaves*. Whitman's poetic lines have the kind of balance and parallelism and resolved paradoxes and echo of cognates and repetition and inversion and many other structural patterns that contribute to make the Bible the great poetry it is.

There is another element of Whitman's background and times that may be traced into his *Leaves*. It appears in the evangelistic fervor of such lines as "O to haste firm holding—to haste, haste on with me" (24), and in such self-dramatization as: "A call in the midst of the crowd, / My own voice, orotund sweeping and final" (59). His was a day of evangelism and oratory. As a child he was no doubt frequently exposed to both. The passionate intimacy and pleading of many lines in *Leaves of Grass* could, with a slightly different emphasis, have been used by an itinerant preacher in his tent-meeting, calling forth the sinners of his audience to be washed in the blood of the Lamb. Other lines could have been declaimed by an orator (Whitman once aspired to make his reputation as one) or politician-patriot envisioning for his audience the glories of America's past and future. Public speaking, or elocution, was one of the fine arts in the nineteenth century.[7]

Ministers and orators prided themselves on their sonorous, rolling periods, their long, musical sentences in which every part fell carefully and rhythmically into place. Initial repetition for dramatic effect and for building toward suspense was usual; frequently speeches built toward a dramatic individual-to-individual appeal or to a frenzied, frantic, apocalyptic, prophetic tone of imminent glory or approaching doom. A change in the words in some of Whitman's most effective passages would ready them for delivery from the nineteenth-century speaker's platform. In the long series of prepositional phrases opening his famous sea-poem,

> Out of the cradle endlessly rocking,
> Out of the mocking-bird's throat, the musical shuttle,
> Out of the Ninth-month midnight,
>
> (180)

phrase is piled on phrase until the whole fantastic structure seems about to collapse, and then the sentence is pulled together by a stop at exactly the right moment of high drama. A different context for the following passage might inspire conversion of the wicked:

Passage to more than India!
O secret of the earth and sky!
Of you O waters of the sea! O winding creeks and rivers!
Of you O woods and fields! of you strong mountains of my land!
Of you O prairies! of you gray rocks!
O morning red! O clouds! O rain and snows!
O day and night, passage to you!

                                                        (294)

It is impossible to touch upon all the elements that might have had
some formative effect upon *Leaves of Grass.* Whitman's Brooklyn days
(as noted in chapter 1) were filled with the opera and the theater. The
opera especially was his passion, and the music, the structure, the libretto—all were absorbed in the gestation of *Leaves.* Not even the poet
could remember all of the books he read or skimmed that might have
added their bit. Nor would it serve much purpose to gather together
all the fragments of the poet's reading to show the resemblances to
lines in *Leaves.* One major influence, however, must not be passed over:
Emerson and transcendentalism. Emerson's response to the 1855 edition of *Leaves*—"it meets the demand I am always making"—suggested
that he saw some kind of fulfillment of his own call for an American
bard. In his essay "The Poet" (1844), Emerson had found no poetry in
America commensurate with the country's or the society's possibilities,
and he prophesied that the American bard would embody his time and
day as well as find his own original relation with the universe. Whitman seemed to fulfill precisely Emerson's demands. He said in one of
his own poems ("Eidólons"):

            The prophet and the bard,
        Shall yet maintain themselves, in higher stages yet,
        Shall mediate to the Modern, to Democracy,
                interpret yet to them,
        God and eidólons.

                                                        (9)

Emerson's oversoul filtered into Whitman's creative vision and hovered
closely over the pages as he wrote.

But when all the influences are counted and weighed, something
still seems to be missing from the "explanation" for *Leaves of Grass.*
Biographers have long sought for the love affair or the comradeship
that set off the spark. In his old age Whitman replied to a query from

the British classical scholar, John Addington Symonds: "My life, young manhood, mid-age, times South, etc., have been jolly bodily, and doubtless open to criticism. Though unmarried, I have had six children—two are dead—one living Southern grandchild—fine boy writes to me occasionally—circumstances (connected with their benefit and fortune) have separated me from intimate relations."[8] This curious "confession," especially when considered in the context of the "Children of Adam" sex poems like "A Woman Waits for Me" and "We Two, How Long We Were Fool'd," has inspired the biographers to create out of their fantasy a Creole romance or a secret love affair that, though briefly and ecstatically fulfilled, could not be sustained—and that provided the tensions that compelled the *Leaves* to grow.[9]

But recent critics have been quick to note that Symonds was pressing Whitman about the "Calamus" poems of comradeship, which in themselves seemed like a different kind of confession:[10] "Here the frailest leaves of me and yet my strongest lasting, / Here I shade and hide my thoughts, I myself do not expose them, / And yet they expose me more than all my other poems" (95). Such statements as these, together with the outright revelation—"(I loved a certain person ardently and my love was not return'd, / Yet out of that I have written these songs.)" (97)—suggested that Whitman's central inspiration experience was not a romance but a close male comradeship, perhaps an earlier relationship like the Washington attachment to Peter Doyle—only more ardent, turbulent, and ambivalent. The complexity of this speculation is indicated when it is recalled that the calamus plant is clearly phallic in its obvious symbolism.

A number of the close male relationships in Whitman's life—with the horse-car conductor Peter Doyle, with Sergeant Thomas P. Sawyer during the Civil War, with Harry Stafford, illiterate son of a farmer at Timber Creek where Whitman spent time outdoors to regain his health in his later years, and with others—have been documented by Whitman's biographers and critics and have revealed that Whitman's attachments to male friends could be as deep and complicated as those between lovers.[11] But no single relationship has been discovered that could mark the beginning of his inspiration as a poet, and it is doubtful that one will be discovered in the future. It is probably a gross simplification, anyway, to explain a literary masterpiece in terms of a single sexual experience or a passing human relationship. It seems more likely that the missing link lies not outside but inside Walt Whitman. The mystery of *Leaves of Grass* can be explained only if the genius of the poet is granted. His most crucial experience was the intimate rendezvous that he kept with his own soul.

I Celebrate Myself

When Whitman opened the first edition of his *Leaves* with the simple declaration, "I Celebrate Myself," he was asserting the theme that was to dominate his book through three editions: 1855, 1856, and 1860. These first three editions of *Leaves of Grass* represent the first unified stage of growth, and the 1860 volume is something of a climax—the first full flowering of the book with its unique structure.

The book that Whitman saw through the press in 1855 was large in format and encased by green covers with an ornate, leafy design. In many ways it was the best size Whitman was to have for any of his editions, for its pages were big enough to allow the full, dramatic, free flow of his long lines without so much bending and twisting back. There appeared first in the book what has come to be known as the 1855 Preface, which in its call for a new "Kosmic" poetry was as revolutionary in its way as the call Wordsworth made for a new diction and emotion in poetry in his 1800 Preface to his *Lyrical Ballads*. There followed twelve untitled poems, all placed under the running title, "Leaves of Grass." On the title page of the book there was no indication of the author, but opposite it was a picture of the vagabond Whitman. If the reader had read far enough into the first poem he would have found this vivid self-portrait of the author:

> Walt Whitman, an American, one of the roughs, a kosmos,
> Disorderly fleshy and sensual . . . . eating drinking and breeding,
> No sentimentalist . . . . no stander above men and women or
>   apart from them . . . . no more modest than immodest.[12]

The twelve poems of the first edition were eventually to get their permanent titles: "Song of Myself," "A Song for Occupations," "To Think of Time," "The Sleepers," "I Sing the Body Electric," "Faces," "Song of the Answerer," "Europe," "A Boston Ballad," "There Was a Child Went Forth," "Who Learns My Lesson Complete," and "Great Are the Myths." All of these poems except the last appeared in the final edition of *Leaves*.

Whitman's instincts were right in rejecting "Great Are the Myths." Although the ideas were clearly his ("The eternal equilibrium of things is great, and the eternal overthrow of things is great, / And there is another paradox"[13]), there seemed to be a curious flagging of imaginative energy in it. By far the best, as well as the longest poem (longer than all the rest put together), was the opening "Song of Myself." Like no other poem in American literature—indeed, unlike any poem ever written before anywhere—this long self-centered and prophetic chant, deliberately physical and aggressively spiritual, seemed designed to shock and startle, surprise and disturb. Placed beside the vagabond portrait of the poet, "Song of Myself" must have seemed to the original audience like the voice of one of the roughs, a "barbaric yawp" sounding "over the roofs of the world."

Although no other poem in the book had quite the force and energy of "Song of Myself," there were lines of great imaginative power scattered throughout all the poems. And two of the remaining poems—the psychological dream-fantasy, "The Sleepers," and the account of poetic-absorption of the universe, "There Was a Child Went Forth"—were among the best Whitman was ever to write. Also running through all the poems, appearing, disappearing, reappearing—like the interweaving melodies of a symphony—were nearly all the themes that were to dominate later editions of *Leaves of Grass*: democracy, science, sexual energy, the driving life-force, death, reconciliation of the great opposed forces of the universe, and many more.

The 1855 edition had a unity of impact that later editions were not to have. The unity appeared, however, not so much in a balancing and arranging of thematic elements as in the image that emerged from all the pages—an image implanted first by the picture of the open-necked, jaunty vagabond of the universe, but reinforced by the impassioned voice behind the daring lines and vibrant words:

> I speak the password primeval . . . . I give the sign of
> democracy;
> By God! I will accept nothing which all cannot have their
> counterpart of on the same terms.[14]

In this poetry was a new man for the New World. Here was a personality created not out of the literary tradition of the past but out of an original relationship with a living time and place. Here, finally, was an *original* American literature from an original tongue.

In hurrying another edition of *Leaves of Grass* through the press, Whitman's main purpose seemed to be to answer Emerson's letter prompted by the 1855 edition. The 1856 edition was small and thick, a cramped book compared with the first edition. Whitman not only used Emerson's "greeting" on the spine of his book, but printed the entire letter at the back and published beside it his delayed and lengthy reply. Although the body of the letter was a revealing proclamation of Whitman's reinvigorated poetic purposes and dedication to such controversial themes as celebration of human sexuality, the opening was embarrassingly fawning in tone: "Here are thirty-two Poems, which I send you, dear Friend and Master, not having found how I could satisfy myself with sending any usual acknowledgment of your letter. The first edition, on which you mailed me that till now unanswered letter, was twelve poems—I printed a thousand copies, and they readily sold; these thirty-two Poems I stereotype, to print several thousand copies of. I much enjoy making poems."[15]

Not only was use of Emerson's letter unauthorized, but there were gross exaggerations in Whitman's reply. The thousand copies of the 1855 edition did not readily sell—indeed, very few copies sold. Whitman exaggerated the sales probably to emphasize his role as the popular, democratic poet. In the 1855 Preface his last words were: "The proof of a poet is that his country absorbs him as affectionately as he has absorbed it" (427). Whitman wanted desperately to be widely acclaimed, and it was but a short step in his imagination to play the role of the popular poet. In his letter to Emerson, he casually predicted: "A few years, and the average annual call for my Poems is ten or twenty thousand copies—more, quite likely."[16] Neither Emerson nor Whitman lived to see such large sales—but the prediction is conservative for our own time.

Twenty new poems, some of Whitman's most powerful, made their initial appearance in the 1856 edition. For the first time the poems were given names, the lead position still given to Whitman's longest poem under its first title—"Poem of Walt Whitman, an American." There was a large number of poems with emphasis on sex. "Poem of the Body" (later, "I Sing the Body Electric") was reprinted from the 1855 edition. New poems related in theme were "Poem of Women" ("Unfolded Out of the Folds"), "Poem of Procreation" ("A Woman Waits for Me"), "Bunch Poem" ("Spontaneous Me"), and "Poem of the Propositions of Nakedness" (later dropped). That this marked emphasis on sex was programmatic on Whitman's part is suggested by the appearance of a justification of the theme in the long letter to Emerson, whereas the 1855 Preface had been relatively silent on the subject.

Whitman wrote to Emerson: "Of bards for These States, if it comes to a question, it is whether they shall celebrate in poems the eternal decency of the amativeness of Nature, the motherhood of all, or whether they shall be the bards of the fashionable delusion of the inherent nastiness of sex, and of the feeble and querulous modesty of deprivation."[17]

Major new poems included "Sun-Down Poem" ("Crossing Brooklyn Ferry"), the Oriental-like chant of spiritual unity lurking through all physical diversity (the poem attracted special praise from Henry David Thoreau[18]); "Poem of the Road" ("Song of the Open Road"), which portrayed in brilliant and engaging imagery the wandering vagabond setting forth on the spiritual journey of life; "Broad-Axe Poem" ("Song of the Broad-Axe"), which expanded the pioneer symbol to embrace the whole of mankind in its infinite diversity of creative struggle; and "Poem of Many in One" ("By Blue Ontario's Shores"), which translated some of the 1855 Preface's prose into poetry calling for American poems to match the grandeur of American geography and ideals. Other new poems that were to find their way into the song section of *Leaves of Grass* were "Poem of Salutation" ("Salut au Monde!") and "Poem of the Sayers of the Words of the Earth" ("A Song of the Rolling Earth").

It was not until the third edition in 1860 that Whitman found a commercial publisher willing to venture the risk of publication— Thayer & Eldridge of Boston. In preparation of this edition Whitman went to Boston and made one of the important decisions of his life. He discussed his book at length with Emerson as the two poets strolled on Boston Common. Emerson was bent on persuading him from publication of the sex poems in the new edition of *Leaves of Grass*. After he had used all of the arguments at his command, he asked what Whitman had to say. After a pause, Whitman replied: "Only that while I can't answer them at all, I feel more settled than ever to adhere to my own theory, and exemplify it."[19]

It was probably Whitman's unwillingness to modify this element of his poetry, so obnoxious to genteel, literary Boston, that caused Emerson to withhold public praise of Whitman and even to deny him admission to an anthology of American poetry that Emerson edited later in his career. Few would now deny that Whitman's instinct was right. And he remained steadfast throughout his career, never once bidding for popularity by bowdlerizing his work or capitulating to the censor, self-appointed or official.

In the 1860 edition Whitman for the first time gave the book a form, a structure that shadowed forth the shape that the book was eventually to assume permanently. The long "Song of Myself" was moved from the initial position and in its place appeared "Proto-Leaf" (later, "Starting from Paumanok"). As its original title suggested, this poem was archetypal for the entire book—the pattern leaf on which all the others were modeled: it presented in embryonic form all of the themes and the major images of the book. Whitman's later additions to the poem indicate that he wanted it to serve as a gathering place and point of departure for all of the melodies on which he was later to work variations. And to balance the proto-leaf, Whitman added at the end of his book a last-leaf in the form of a farewell poem, "So Long!" In this poem he again went lightly over all his major themes, but they were muted, mellowed in the fading light of the sad separation—the author from the reader.

Between these poems of hail and farewell, Whitman filled out a large book, adding a total of 124 new poems. He hit upon a new and happy idea of placing his thematically related poems in clusters; and he was to experiment with this idea in all future editions, shifting poems from cluster to cluster, and shifting the clusters to various positions, until he intuitively discovered the precisely right order for all his poems—where in their mutual and multiple reflections they intensified their meanings in their reverberations with each other. In the 1860 edition appeared a number of experimental clusters—"Chants Democratic," "Messenger Leaves," "Thoughts"—that were later abandoned. But two clusters appeared that were to become two of the most celebrated sections of *Leaves of Grass*: "Enfans d'Adam" (later, "Children of Adam") and "Calamus." Into the first of these sections Whitman brought together his sex lyrics, the poems of procreation, celebrating the act of generation as a symbol of man's involvement in mystic evolution. In the second cluster, clearly companion to the first, Whitman gathered together a number of new poems celebrating "manly attachment," comradeship, and democratic brotherhood. In spite of the criticism they aroused, these clusters remained in all future editions of *Leaves of Grass*.

Two sea poems that appeared in the 1860 edition have, because of their seemingly personal nature, caused much speculation as to their origin and their hidden or symbolic meaning. "As I Ebb'd with the Ocean of Life," with its tone of resignation bordering on despair ("I too am but a trail of drift and debris" [186]), injected a new attitude in *Leaves of Grass*—in sharp contrast with the expansive egotism of earlier editions. But the best new poem, and one of the greatest of any

Whitman ever wrote, was "A Word Out of the Sea" ("Out of the Cradle Endlessly Rocking"). This narrative reminiscence of a childhood experience, with its drama of the boy as outsetting bard listening by the seaside to the mockingbird's carol of lonesome love and the sea's answering hiss of "death," seems to be a veiled treatment of some personal love-tragedy of the poet. But though the poem does have a note of personal anguish and presents symbols that tempt the reader to guess at a personal application, no biographer has yet successfully solved the riddle the poem seems to pose. This failure, however, has not deprived the poem of its proper position among the three or four of Whitman's best.

Beat! Beat! Drums!

The second phase in the growth of *Leaves of Grass* witnessed more changes in plan and structure than creation of new poems. The fourth edition appeared after the Civil War in 1867 (*Drum-Taps* had appeared separately in 1865), and it served as the basis for the English edition of 1868. In the fifth edition, published in 1871–72, Whitman appeared to have resolved a number of the problems that had made the previous edition somewhat unsatisfactory. He seemed once more to have his past work firmly under control and his future plans well laid.

The 1867 edition, in many ways the most chaotic of all the editions, showed that Whitman had been doing a great deal of revision. There were deletions as well as transfers and changes. For example, the "Calamus" section underwent some major modifications, with the actual dropping of three of the most personal of the poems of "manly attachment": "Long I Thought that Knowledge Alone Would Suffice" (no. 8), "Hours Continuing Long, Sore, and Heavy-Hearted" (no. 9), and "Who Is Now Reading This?" (no. 16). A new poem was written for the opening of the book—"Inscription" (later, "One's-Self I Sing"). This short poem, to stand at the beginning of all later editions, was a succinct statement of the poet's intention to sing "of Life immense in passion, pulse, and power." All in all, this edition gives the impression of having been put to press before the poet had made up his mind about a number of structural problems—while his imagination and poetry were still in a state of flux. The "Drum-Taps" poems and the "Sequel" containing the Lincoln elegy were simply stuffed in at the end of the volume, still in the separate pagination given them when they were published by themselves.

In many ways more significant than the American fourth edition was the British edition based on it, published in 1868. Although this edition does not legitimately represent a stage in the growth of *Leaves*—Whitman had no hand in arranging and shaping it—it did play an important part in the growth of the poet's reputation abroad. In England Whitman was much more successful than in America in attracting support from the established literary groups. William Michael Rossetti, who edited the volume, managed to leave out the poems most likely to offend because of their excessive sexuality. He introduced it with high praise and thus sent it forth with much stronger support than the *Leaves* had ever been published with in this country (except, perhaps, for the unauthorized Emersonian publicity of the 1856 edition). The volume, which attracted wide and sympathetic attention, was the object of high praise by such distinguished poets as Algernon Swinburne. Swinburne's later attack on Whitman, made after he had read all of the *Leaves* and particularly the poems of procreation, could not decrease the impact of his earlier rhapsodic approval.[20]

Like the fourth edition, the fifth edition of 1871–72 showed signs of a good deal of poetic activity, particularly of revision and of shifting of poems. The single introductory poem "Inscription" became the nucleus for a cluster of poems that combined greetings with glimpses of themes and images to come—all under the title "Inscriptions." For the first time "Drum-Taps" and the Lincoln poems found a permanent place within the *Leaves.* Whitman had come to see that his emotional experiences of the Civil War, though by no means identical with his pre–Civil War feelings and attitudes, were in fact complementary. It is not so much that Whitman changed his conception of his book as that he expanded it to include what rightfully belonged—what was different only on the surface.

That Whitman considered the 1871–72 edition complete and finished is suggested by a preface that he wrote for an 1872 pamphlet publication of "As a Strong Bird on Pinions Free" (later, "Thou Mother with Thy Equal Brood"). He said: *"Leaves of Grass,* already publish'd, is, in its intentions, the song of a great composite *democratic individual,* male or female. And following on and amplifying the same purpose, I suppose I have in my mind to run through the chants of this volume (if ever completed), the thread-voice, more or less audible, of an aggregated, inseparable, unprecedent, vast, composite, electric *democratic nationality"* (432). Uncertainty of intent seems to lurk behind every word of this statement; and well might Whitman have been uncertain. Although the 1871–72 edition had found a place for the war and Lincoln poems, it had carried as an annex a large number of poems under the title "Passage to India." These poems, with their emphasis on death and spirituality, had not yet found a true place in the *Leaves*; they had simply been stuck in the back of the book. Whitman seemed vaguely aware that they belonged, but he did not seem to know where.

Ye Aged Fierce Enigmas

The final stage in the growth of *Leaves* entailed the appearance of the four books by that title in 1876, 1881–82, 1889, and 1891–92, only one of which can properly be called a *new* edition—that of 1881–82; the others were simply reprintings from the same plates as previous editions. Thus, for all practical purposes, the sixth edition of 1881–82 represented the climax in the life of the book. In it *Leaves of Grass* achieved its lasting shape and permanent personality.

The so-called Centennial Edition of 1876 consisted of two volumes, the first reprinting the 1871 edition of *Leaves of Grass* and the second, entitled *Two Rivulets,* including the "Passage to India" poems that had appeared under separate pagination at the end of the 1872 reprint of the 1871 volume. In addition, *Two Rivulets* gathered together, sometimes without even changing the pagination, all of Whitman's miscellaneous publications, including his prose. The Preface that he wrote for this volume indicated that his plans as announced in the 1872 Preface no longer were at the fore-front of his imagination. Instead, he was filled with thoughts of another theme and still another companion volume to *Leaves* that he wanted to write:

It was originally my intention after chanting in *Leaves of Grass* the songs of the Body and Existence, to then compose a further, equally needed Volume, based on those convictions of perpetuity and conservation which, enveloping all precedents, make the unseen Soul absolutely at last. I meant, while in a sort continuing the theme of my first chants, to shift the slides, and exhibit the problem and paradox of the same ardent and fully appointed Personality entering the sphere of the resistless gravitation of Spiritual Law, and with cheerful face estimating Death, not at all as the cessation, but as somehow what I feel it must be, the entrance upon by far the greatest part of existence, and something that Life is at least as much for, as it is for itself. (434)

Whitman's plundering of the *Leaves* volume to concentrate his spiritual and death poems in "Passage to India" left the *Leaves* in one of its weakest states.

It is difficult to say what happened between 1876 and 1881 to enable Whitman to discover at last the form that he had sought so long, particularly in view of his 1876 experiment in drastically reshuffling the poems. Whatever it was, it lasted out his life, for he never changed the basic pattern he adopted for the 1881 edition. No longer did he hold back a group of poems to serve as a nucleus about which he hoped to construct a companion volume to his *Leaves*. For the first time he saw that all of his poems fit, in some way, into his overall scheme. It must, however, again be emphasized that he did not alter his vision but expanded it to embrace poems that did not before seem to belong. For the first time, all of the "Passage to India" poems found their thematic position in the basic *Leaves*, the poem of that title placed in the latter part of the book where by its magnetism as one of Whitman's most powerful poems it attracted about itself a cluster of highly spiritual, "religious" poems, poems that tackled the "aged fierce enigmas" that have baffled men of all times and places.

With the absorption by *Leaves* of the "Passage to India" poems, the third and final stage of its growth was completed. And Whitman looked upon the structure as filled out and finished. When he looked back over his career in "A Backward Glance O'er Travel'd Roads," reviewing his "unconscious, or mostly unconscious" intentions, he could discover a purpose that had come to fulfillment and fruition: "This was a feeling or ambition to articulate and faithfully express in literary or poetic form, and uncompromisingly, my own physical, emotional, moral, intellectual, and aesthetic Personality, in the midst of, and tallying, the momentous spirit and facts of its immediate days, and of current America—and to exploit that Personality, identified with place and date, in a far more candid and comprehensive sense than any hitherto poem or book" (444). This was a single and unified purpose, broad enough, he understood at last, to embrace all of the poems he wrote. No companion volume was needed.

The two remaining publications of *Leaves* displayed embellishments, but they were essentially the 1881 edition reissued. The 1889 issue was a fancy one that included many portraits of the poet, but its only real change from the sixth edition was the addition of an Annex, clearly separate from the main structure of *Leaves*, consisting of miscellaneous poems under the title "Sands at Seventy." As a prose commentary on his poetry, Whitman concluded his book with the nostalgic and perceptive "A Backward Glance O'er Travel'd Roads." The so-called Deathbed Edition of 1891–92 added to the 1889 issue only another Annex of old-age poems—"Good-Bye My Fancy." Beginning in 1897 there was added to the Deathbed Edition still another Annex, "Old Age Echoes"; these were the very last poems gathered together at Whitman's request by his literary executors and under a title supplied by the poet.

Whitman wrote in a prefatory note to the Deathbed Edition: "As there are now several editions of L. of G., different texts and dates, I wish to say that I prefer and recommend this present one, complete, for future printing, if there should be any; a copy and fac-simile, indeed, of the text of these 438 pages. The subsequent adjusting interval which is so important to form'd and launch'd works, books especially, has pass'd; and waiting till fully after that, I have given . . . my concluding words" (1). His reference is, of course, to "A Backward Glance." Whitman's self-assurance that the structure of *Leaves* embodied his vision is suggested by his permitting it, after some twenty-five years of constant revision, to stand unchanged for the last ten years of his life. That he wanted that structure preserved and perpetuated is certain from this deathbed charge he made to the future.

Chapter Three
A Poetics for Democracy

Whitman spent a lifetime writing one book, and he poured into that one book all the prime resources of his spirit and imagination. The other scattered pieces written by Whitman have interest only as they relate to *Leaves of Grass*. And a surprising number of them relate directly. In his most memorable prose, Whitman was concerned primarily with working out a poetics for America, a new theory of poetry for the New World democracy. In talking about poetry in his prose, Whitman was merely extending the discussion from his poetry; for in poem after poem he discussed a democratic poetics or dramatized himself as the New World poet.

There is a marked contrast between Whitman's pre–*Leaves of Grass* journalistic prose and the prose that he wrote beginning with the appearance of his masterpiece. In his newspaper pieces he is clear, lucid, grammatical, proper, conventional—and frequently dull. In the later prose, Whitman is murky, tortured, ambiguous, involuted—and often profound. It is as though he threw away his pen in 1855 and began to write with the gnarled twig of an ancient oak. Whitman's main arguments on poetics may be traced through a series of his most pertinent pieces: (1) 1855 Preface; (2) 1856 letter to Emerson and three reviews of *Leaves*; (3) 1871 *Democratic Vistas*; (4) 1872 Preface to *As a Strong Bird on Pinions Free*; (5) 1876 Preface to *Two Rivulets*; (6) 1882 *Specimen Days*; (7) 1888 "A Backward Glance O'er Travel'd Roads."

There is a good deal of prose beyond these seven items. But of course most of the journalism of the early days can be set aside as not directly related to Whitman's main interests in *Leaves of Grass*. Later prose, particularly the prose of Whitman's old age, tends to be miscellaneous and is noteworthy only as it involves particular subjects of interest. Whitman's letters sometimes fill in some large gaps—for example, his letters to Peter Doyle published as *Calamus* (1897) and his Civil War letters to his mother published as *The Wound-Dresser* (1898). A number of volumes of miscellaneous pieces are of course invaluable to the student intending comprehensive study of the poet: *Notes and Fragments* (1904), *The Uncollected Poetry and Prose of Walt Whitman* (1921), and

Walt Whitman's Workshop (1928). These and other such volumes, together with much previously unpublished material, have been gathered into a total of nine volumes in *The Collected Writings of Walt Whitman*: three volumes entitled *Day-books and Notebooks,* edited by William White (1978); and six volumes under the general title *Notebooks and Unpublished Prose Manuscripts,* edited by Edward F. Grier (1984).

Indeed, any critical survey of Whitman's work would almost necessarily conclude that only three essays are of sufficient independent vitality and interest to claim for Whitman a lasting (if small) reputation in prose: the 1855 Preface, *Democratic Vistas,* and "A Backward Glance."

The importance of the 1855 Preface is in part historical, providing as it does a kind of manifesto from which Americans can honestly date their literary independence. But it is more than simply a point of pride. The Preface is a rough-hewn outline, with all the simplicity and strength and originality and nativeness of a sturdy log cabin, by which America might measure her cosmic poets to come. The Preface provided Americans with an attitude, a faith, and a vision. After reading it, they were finally prepared to recognize native genius, to distinguish it finally from all the imitations of foreign models. Here delineated in full were the subjects for poets, the attributes of the poet, the characteristics of poems, the involvements of the audience—all detailed in a rough, vigorous, masculine prose. Perhaps the greatest achievement in the essay is, in spite of calling for an American poetry, its essential escape from narrow provincialism: Whitman insisted throughout that the poet must first be cosmic before he can be American.

Democratic Vistas may seem at first glance to be a political piece, but deeper reading reveals it as another impassioned plea for a great literature. Of all Whitman's prose, however, *Democratic Vistas* is certainly the most likely to provide Whitman a reputation as an essayist independent of his fame as a poet. It consists of three major parts. The first offers a survey of American democracy as it in actuality is in the "mass." And what Whitman pictures—the "depravity of the business classes"—provides a harsh indictment that is only partly redeemed by his recollection of the unselfish and even heroic action of the citizenry during the Civil War. The second part outlines the balance and counterpoise of the "mass" in the democracy—that element which, if atrophied, could mean democracy's downfall: individualism. Whitman becomes lyrical in his call for a "rich, luxuriant, varied personalism" as the very foundation on which democratic civilization must rest. In the third and climactic part of his essay, Whitman calls for an "American imaginative literature," endowed with "grand and archetypal models," that will support and buttress a "new and grater personalism." Literature can, in short, make the democratic vista a reality: "I say that democracy can never prove itself beyond cavil, until it founds and luxuriantly grows its own forms of art, poems, schools, theology, displacing all that exists, or that has been produced anywhere in the past, under opposite influences" (457).

"A Backward Glance O'er Travel'd Roads," written at the end of Whitman's career, serves as counterpoint to the 1855 Preface, written at the beginning. In this essay Whitman makes a frank assessment of his achievement in the light of his intentions and plans: "Result of seven or eight stages and struggles extending through nearly thirty years, (as I nigh my three-score-and-ten I live largely on memory,) I look upon *Leaves of Grass,* now finish'd to the end of its opportunities and powers, as my definitive *carte visite* to the coming generations of the New World" (443). Whitman's backward glance is mainly directed at the major themes of his *Leaves*: procreation, science, democracy, individuality, the Civil War, spirituality. From the vantage point of his old age, all of these diverse themes and others fit together comfortably and compatibly in the grand scheme of the book—now abandoned to the world.

Whitman's prose in its composite whole provided a poetics for democracy. It is useful to sort out the elements of that poetics as another way of understanding Whitman's experiments and purposes, intentions and achievements, in *Leaves of Grass*. Whitman was constantly concerned about the proper relationship between the poet and reality, and the proper province of poetry. He frequently discussed the various attributes of the poet. He dealt at length with the several elements in poetry and the problems of making poems. And he spoke often of the responsibilities of the poet's audience. Each of these subjects provides a point around which to cluster Whitman's ideas.[1]

The Province of Poetry

Whitman said in 1855, "What I experience or portray shall go from my composition without a shred of my composition. You shall stand by my side and look in the mirror with me" (418). The use of the mirror image[2] seemed almost unconscious, quickly sought out to reinforce the dominant idea that Whitman would not, through literary frills, stand between his work and the reader. Perhaps the very casualness with which Whitman used the mirror image is an indication of how easily he took for granted the representational theory of art. In any case, his major ideas about the nature of literature were based on his version of the representational theory.

As suggested by his use of the mirror metaphor, Whitman assumed throughout all of his commentary on literature that there was not only an important but a crucial relationship between poetry and life: the poet's task was to represent reality in his poem; the reader judged the poem by comparing it to the world. But Whitman did not conceive of art as representational in any superficial sense. Inasmuch as the mirror implied *surface* reflection or imitation, it was woefully inadequate and even misleading. Whitman did not hide his contempt for the merely imitative; in *Democratic Vistas* he called for a "new founded" literature which did not "merely . . . copy and reflect existing surfaces" and he called for an end to the "useless attempt to repeat the material creation by daguerreotyping the exact likeness by mortal mental means" (496).

In view of this strong denunciation of imitating or daguerreotyping, it is fair to raise the question as to what Whitman expected his reader to see when he stood by the poet to look in the mirror. The secret was, of course, that the poet's mirror was endowed with magical qualities that allowed it to penetrate beneath the surface into the secret of things:

> The noiseless myriads,
> The infinite oceans where the rivers empty,
> The separate countless free identities, like eyesight,
> The true realities, eidólons.
>
> (9)

The "true realities," what Whitman (along with many mystics) elsewhere called the "real realities," were the spiritual manifestations or counterparts of all material objects. The spiritual world in which the eidólons reside could not, of course, be known through the ordinary senses. If the poet's mirror did not somehow reflect this spirituality of the external, sensuous world, it was merely reflecting surfaces that could never be the substance of true poetry.

When Whitman proclaimed in the opening poem of *Leaves of Grass,* "The Modern Man I Sing," he was fulfilling a cardinal tenet in his poetic theory (1855 Preface): "The direct trial of him who would be the greatest poet is today. If he does not flood himself with the immediate age as with vast oceanic tides . . . and if he be not himself the age transfigured . . . let him merge in the general run and wait his development" (424–25). Whitman was not, of course, asking for celebration of the nineteenth century above both the past and the future. He was merely stating what was for him the simple truth: the mirror of the poet could not reflect a dead past. The dictum of the transcendent significance of the *now* was as true, in Whitman's view, for a poet of three hundred years ago or three hundred years hence as it was for the poet of his day. Behind this theory was the assumption of the creative virility of the poet immersed, "as with vast oceanic tides," in the experiences of life (experiences which must be "now," never past or future) as opposed to the creative sterility of the poet withdrawn, disengaged from the current experience, finding an illusory reality in times departed or yet to come.

The artist, thought Whitman, should respectfully peruse and then dismiss the past. And he should dismiss it and stand in his own "place" and with his "own day" not because the past was inferior ("nothing can ever be greater" [16]), but because the poet's task was to mirror reality. The past could not be mirrored simply because it was past. The present was therefore the only possible subject for the true poet. And the present in nineteenth-century America, Whitman translated into two essential aspects, science and democracy. Whitman's view of history was both chronological and spatial. Man's record, he believed, could be divided into three great periods that corresponded to three geographical areas: the age of myth and fable (the age of "budding bibles"), centered in Asia; the age of feudalism, in Europe; and the age of science and democracy, in America. Science he invariably opposed to fable and myth; democracy to feudalism.

In *Democratic Vistas* Whitman wrote: "Note, today an instructive, curious spectacle and conflict. Science, (twin, in its fields, of Democracy in its)—Science, testing absolutely all thoughts, all works, has already burst well upon the world—a sun, mounting, most illuminating, most glorious—surely never again to set. But against it, deeply entrench'd, holding possession, yet remains (not only through the churches and schools, but by imaginative literature, and unregenerate poetry), the fossil theology of the mythic-materialistic, superstitious, untaught and credulous, fable-loving, primitive ages of humanity" (489). It is indeed curious that Whitman felt compelled, in his vivid image of the science as sun, to assert that this science-sun is "surely never again to set." Such assertion (indeed, what sun has never set?) seemed to spring from an uneasy certainty that science was the nineteenth century's myth.[3] In "A Backward Glance O'er Travel'd Roads," Whitman seemed to admit that he had substituted a contemporary myth for that of the past, but he did not admit that his myth was inferior to that which preceded it: "Modern science and democracy seem'd to be throwing out their challenge to poetry to put them in its statements in contradistinction to the songs and myths of the past. As I see now (perhaps too late), I have unwittingly taken up that challenge and made an attempt at such statements—which I certainly would not assume to do now, knowing more clearly what it means" (444–45).

Although Whitman insisted on the poet's faithfulness to reality, and in his century and country saw that reality consisted of science and democracy, he was far from demanding that all true poets should choose as their subject matter astronomy, biology, and politics. Whitman's own phrase ("their construction underlies the structure of every perfect poem" [419]) suggested the ideal relationship between the twin suns and poetry. Science and democracy were not the sole subjects for the poet but rather constituted the appropriate modern frame of reference; the poet who ignored or denied this frame retreated to the past. In this view, literary works of the past were not inferior but were enclosed (and perhaps limited) by a different frame of reference ("A Backward Glance"): "Just as all the old imaginative works rest, after their kind, on long trains of presuppositions, often entirely unmention'd by themselves, . . . so *Leaves of Grass* . . . presupposed something different from any other, and, as it stands, is the result of such presupposition" (446).

Whitman saw that the contemporary success of poets was no clue to their genius and worth (*Democratic Vistas*): "Today, in books, in the rivalry of writers, especially novelists, success . . . is for him or her who strikes the mean flat average, the sensational appetite for stimulus, incident, persifilage, &c., and depicts, to the common calibre, sensual, exterior life. To such . . . the audiences are limitless and profitable; but they cease presently. While this day, or any day, to workmen portraying interior or spiritual life, the audiences were limited, and often laggard—but they last forever" (488). That "proper dwelling" for the poet, to which the facts of science provided the entrance, was this "interior or spiritual life," and it was this life, the unseen but no less real, that Whitman attempted to mirror; moreover, his faith in this world motivated his claim to be a poet of religion. He wrote in the 1872 Preface: "When I commenced, years ago, elaborating the plan of my poems, and continued turning over that plan, . . . one deep purpose underlay the others, and has underlain it and its execution ever since—and that has been the Religious purpose" (431). This "Religious purpose" was to mirror a reality that had its proof not in the eyesight or intellect, but in the spirit and soul. Whitman explained in "A Backward Glance": "While I cannot understand it or argue it out, I fully believe in a clue and purpose in Nature, entire and several; and that invisible spiritual results, just as real and definite as the visible, eventuate all concrete life and all materialism, through Time" (453).

Whitman's insistence that science and democracy, as the realities of nineteenth-century America, "furnish the prevading atmosphere" of poems, has brought him the titles "poet of science" and "poet of democracy."[4] The latter has probably been given him by critics more frequently than the former. Yet no one claims that Whitman adopted as his main subject matter in his poetry either science or democracy. If Whitman himself were to assent to be the poet of something, he would probably insist (as he insisted again and again in his prose) on being the poet of religion.[5] But none of these labels seems fitting when tested by Whitman's great poems—"Song of Myself," "Crossing Brooklyn Ferry," "Out of the Cradle Endlessly Rocking," "When Lilacs Last in the Dooryard Bloom'd." In insisting that science, democracy, and, above them, religion (or spirituality) must underlie the structure of modern poems, Whitman was not limiting the possible subjects of poetry ("A Backward Glance": "The Poetic area is very spacious—has room for all—has so many mansions!" [450]); he was instead defining the nineteenth century's view of the universe and itself in which the poet must be immersed if he is to be a poet of the modern, as Homer was immersed in his time by embracing Greek "mythology," and Shakespeare in his by reflecting "feudalism." Whitman did not ask the poet to propagandize but rather to embody or "presuppose" the modern "myth" of science, democracy, and, above all, spirituality.

Attributes of the Poet

In speaking of the function of the ideal poet, if Whitman frequently used the words *mirrors, channels, represents, portrays, depicts, delineates,* he also frequently used *embodies, encloses, expresses.* These latter terms suggest that he visualized the poet's role not only as *imitator* of the real reality of nature, but also as *illuminator.* He said in the 1855 Preface: "The greatest poet does not only dazzle his rays over character and scenes and passions . . . he finally ascends and finishes all . . . he exhibits the pinnacles that no man can tell what they are for or what is beyond . . . he glows a moment on the extremest verge" (417). The poet glowing on the "extremest verge" is surely the same poet who mirrors the *internal* reality, but Whitman invoked both images, suggesting a fusion of qualities: not only is there an *internal* spirituality in the makeup of the universe but the poet must be specially endowed to discover and exhibit it: "As they [poets of the cosmos] emit themselves facts are showered over with light . . . the daylight is lit with more volatile light . . . also the deep between the setting and rising sun goes deeper many fold" (421).

What is the source of the poet's flamelike light that illuminates the dark and hidden corners of the universe? The answer is not easy to find in Whitman's intricate prose; but one of the most curious passages (from the 1855 Preface) in all his work presents a startling image that sheds some light on the source of the poet's power of insight: "Extreme caution or prudence, the soundest organic health, large hope and comparison and fondness for women and children, large alimentiveness and destructiveness and causality, with a perfect sense of the oneness of nature and the propriety of the same spirit applied to human affairs . . . these are called up of the float of the brain of the world to be parts of the greatest poet from his birth out of his mother's womb and from her birth and of her mother's" (422). The strange and even astonishing vocabulary in this passage presents some baffling problems until one realizes that Whitman was displaying a knowledge of the "new" or "advanced" psychology of his day—phrenology. His own chart of bumps, which he had displayed in one of the anonymous reviews he wrote for the first edition of *Leaves* (see chapter 1) indicated that he was highly developed in most of the traits he listed here for the "greatest poet."

But the entire passage focuses on the striking image, "the float of the brain of the world." Like the chemical figure in "Crossing Brooklyn Ferry" ("I too had been struck from the float forever held in solution" [118]), the image seems a concrete representation of Emerson's oversoul. But in shifting from spirit to mind (or soul to brain), Whitman seems to foreshadow some such concept as the collective unconscious of C. G. Jung. The mind of the greatest poet, formed from qualities "called up" from the world's great archetypal or primordial brain, will naturally be endowed with an acute and universal perceptiveness and will sense "the oneness of nature."

Whitman seemed to feel that if he could name the poet, find the right epithet for him, the people would recognize him. Referring to America, he said (1855 Preface): "Their Presidents shall not be their common referee so much as their poets shall. Of all mankind the great poet is the equable man. . . . He is the arbiter of the diverse and he is the key. He is the equalizer of his age and land . . . he supplies what wants supplying and checks what wants checking" (414). *Referee, arbiter, key, equalizer*—the poet is all of these and also more: "The known universe has one complete lover and that is the greatest poet" (416). But the epithet which has proved most popular with Whitman's critics is *prophet*: "He [the poet] is a seer . . . he is individual . . . he is complete in himself . . . the others are as good as he, only he sees it and they do not" (415).

When Whitman called the poet *seer*, he did not mean prognosticator (1855 Preface): "What the eyesight does to the rest he [the poet] does to the rest. Who knows the curious mystery of the eyesight? The other senses corroborate themselves, but this is removed from any proof but its own and foreruns the identities of the spiritual world" (415). The metaphor of the eyesight suggests that the poet, in his role as prophet, sees into the spiritual heart of things for the rest of mankind. The poet, endowed with a transcendent sight, serves as humanity's eyes of the spirit. If the poet foresees the future, it is not through supernatural gift but rather through a sensitive and perceptive interpretation of what is and what went before: "Past and present and future are not disjoined but joined. The greatest poet forms the consistence of what is to be from what has been and is . . . he places himself where the future becomes present" (417).

If Whitman's view of the poet as seer has been overemphasized, his concept of the poet as priest has been generally under-stressed. In the 1855 Preface, Whitman said, "There will soon be no more priests. Their work is done. . . . Through the divinity of themselves shall the kosmos and the new breed of poets be interpreters of men and women and of all events and things. They shall find their inspiration in real objects today, symptoms of the past and future . . . They shall not deign to defend immortality or God or the perfection of things or liberty or the exquisite beauty and reality of the soul" (425–26). Whitman never abandoned this view of the poet as self-poised priest. In

Democratic Vistas he announced, "The priest departs, the divine literatus comes" (457). Probably the most extreme representation of this view appeared in "Passage to India," in which the poet was elevated from priest to the position of Christ:

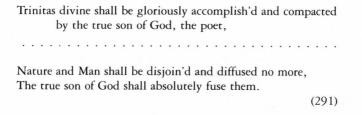

> Trinitas divine shall be gloriously accomplish'd and compacted
>   by the true son of God, the poet,
>
> . . . .
>
> Nature and Man shall be disjoin'd and diffused no more,
> The true son of God shall absolutely fuse them.
>
> (291)

Referee, key, prophet, or priest, it is clear that Whitman's poet writes because he feels a compulsion to do so. Throughout *Leaves of Grass* recur images of the overflowing container or the smoldering fire. Whitman announced in "Starting from Paumanok":

> I will therefore let flame from me the burning fires that
>   were threatening to consume me,
> I will lift what has too long kept down those smouldering
>   fires,
>
> (17)

The vivid imagery here suggests the importance of the emotions—and turbulent emotions at that—to the creation of poetry. Whitman exclaimed in "Song of Myself": "I know perfectly well my own egotism, / Know my omnivorous lines and must not write any less" (60). Such statements frequently encountered in *Leaves of Grass* make clear that the true poet has no choice—he writes because he *must,* because he cannot escape his own furious compulsion.

Though Whitman knew his own egotism, his poetry is not essentially a poetry consumed with the personal. In spite of its apparent emphasis on the self of the poet, his poetry is basically dramatic. The "I" in any one Whitman poem is not so much a personal reference as a fusion of several characters, a composite character, who exists no place other than in the poem. Whitman early suggested, in one of his anonymous reviews of the 1855 edition of *Leaves of Grass,* his motives for focusing attention on *self* in his poetry: "Other poets celebrate great events, personages, romances, wars, loves, passions, the victories and power of their country, or some real or imagined incident—and polish their work and come to conclusions, and satisfy the reader. This poet [Whitman] celebrates natural propensities in himself; and that is the way he celebrates all."[6]

Whitman apparently never deviated from this purpose of celebrating all through celebrating self. In 1872, he could even envision the hero of his book as omnisexual: *"Leaves of Grass* . . . is, in its intentions, the song of a great composite *democratic individual,* male or female" (432). The "I" of his poetry may be a dramatization of the typical American, or the Cosmic Poet; a dramatization of a soldier on the battlefield, or of a comet rushing through the heavens. Whatever it may be and is, the "I" is always something more—and something less—than the historical Walt Whitman.

The Making of Poems

Whitman's respect for the complexity of artistic principles is suggested by his brilliant and illuminating image of the chess game (*Specimen Days*): "The play of Imagination, with the sensuous objects of Nature for symbols and Faith—with Love and Pride as the unseen impetus and moving-power of all, make up the curious chess-game of a poem."[7] No romantic who genuinely believed in the prevailing "automatic" writing theories would ever have conceived the writing of a poem in terms of the strategy planned and followed in a game of chess. Yet many critics have, without reservation, identified Whitman with the romantic school of "automatic" writers.[8]

No doubt Whitman through his poetry contributed to the general belief that he viewed the poet as mere passive agent who wrote automatically, perhaps even in trance, what came from some external and divine source. When one becomes caught up in the hypnotic chant of the poet, and lost in the poet's wild abandon, the "automatic" writing theory seems to have its finest example in Whitman. It requires a somewhat distant perspective to realize, however, that there is in Whitman's poetry, as in all other great poetry, a vast difference between effect and cause: the effect of lawlessness is not, as frequently assumed, achieved by the poet's real abandon; such an effect is achieved only by the poet's strictest artistic control. Genuine lawlessness could result in nothing but bad poetry. Whitman once wrote to William D. O'Connor: "It [*Drum-Taps*] is in my opinion superior to *Leaves of Grass*—certainly more perfect as a work of art, being adjusted in all

its proportions, & its passion having the indispensable merit that
though to the ordinary reader, let loose with wildest abandon, the true
artist can see it is yet under control."[9] This statement is perhaps more
revealing of Whitman's discipline as a poet than any other remark he
made.

In his obsession with "sensuous objects," not only in theory but also
in practice, Whitman was in a sense a forerunner of the imagists. He
confessed, in a brilliant short poem, his almost childlike ecstasy in
sensuous contact with *things*:

> Beginning my studies the first step pleas'd me so much,
> The mere fact consciousness, these forms, the power of motion,
> The least insect or animal, the senses, eyesight, love,
> The first step I say awed me and pleas'd me so much,
> I have hardly gone and hardly wish'd to go any farther,
> But stop and loiter all the time to sing it in ecstatic songs.
>
> (10)

Whitman's famous catalogs are in reality brief or extended imagist
poems. Image follows image in such pell-mell rush that the reader,
glutted with the concrete, pants for a generalization. But Whitman
reminded himself that the poet's duty bade him go beyond the concrete
object (1855 Preface): "The land and sea, the animals fishes and birds,
the sky of heaven and the orbs, the forests mountains and rivers, are
not small themes . . . but folks expect of the poet to indicate more
than the beauty and dignity which always attach to dumb real objects
. . . they expect him to indicate the path between reality and their
souls" (415). Whitman's constant faith was that somehow, someway,
the material universe held the clue to the spiritual, and that impassioned encounter with the one would lead to knowledge and apprehension of the other.

Related to Whitman's belief in the ultimate spiritual reality of all
things was perhaps the leading tenet of his principles of art—suggestiveness (1876 Preface): "In certain parts, in these flights [*Leaves of
Grass* and *Two Rivulets*], or attempting to depict or suggest them, I
have not been afraid of the charge of obscurity . . . because human
thought, poetry or melody, must leave dim escapes and outlets—must
possess a certain fluid, aerial character, akin to space itself, obscure to
those of little or no imagination, but indispensable to the highest purposes" (440). Then (as now) the answer to the charge of obscurity was

that the fault may as well rest in the reader as in the poem. For those who were irritated by the indefinite or indirect, and demanded to know the "meaning" of a poem, Whitman had little sympathy (*Specimen Days*): "Common teachers or critics are always asking 'What does it mean?' Symphony of fine musician, or sunset, or sea-waves rolling up the beach—what do they mean? Undoubtedly in the most subtle-elusive sense they mean something—as love does, and religion does, and the best poem;—but who shall fathom and define those meanings?"[10]

Whitman's concept of organic form is probably the best known of his poetic principles. He gave his pronouncements the ring of authority (1855 Preface): "The pleasure of poems is not in them that take the handsomest measure and similes and sound" (417); "The poetic quality is not marshalled in rhyme or uniformity or abstract addresses to things nor in melancholy complaints or good precepts, but is the life of these and much else and is in the soul. . . . Who troubles himself about his ornaments or fluency is lost" (415). In these passages Whitman was echoing Emerson's famous dictum, "For it is not metres, but a metre-making argument that makes a poem,—a thought so passionate and alive that like the spirit of a plant or an animal it has an architecture of its own, and adorns nature with a new thing."[11]

A part of Whitman's disdain for ornaments sprang from his desire to mirror the unvarnished truth of nature (1855 Preface): "He [the greatest poet] swears to his art, I will not be meddlesome, I will not have in my writing any elegance or effect or originality to hang in the way between me and the rest like curtains. I will have nothing hang in the way, not the richest curtains" (417–18). This passage could be read as a plea for functional over ornamental metaphor. Ornaments that are their own excuse for being are not to be tolerated; only those that aid the poet in his task of representation are to be allowed (1855 Preface): "The rhyme and uniformity of perfect poems show the free growth of metrical laws and bud from them as unerringly and loosely as lilacs or roses on a bush, and take shapes as compact as the shapes of chestnuts and oranges and melons and pears, and shed the perfume impalpable to form. The fluency and ornaments of the finest poems or music or orations or recitations are not independent but dependent" (415). "The English language," Whitman said (1855 Preface), "befriends the grand American expression . . . it is brawny enough and limber and full enough. On the tough stock of a race who through all change of circumstances was never without the idea of political liberty, which is the animus of all liberty, it has attracted the terms of daintier and gayer and subtler and more elegant tongues" (426). Such statements suggest Whitman's comprehensive understanding of his artistic medium. In old age, he once remarked to Horace Traubel, "This subject of language interests me—interests me: I never quite get it out of my mind. I sometimes think the *Leaves* is only a language experiment—that it is an attempt to give the spirit, the body, the man, new words, new potentialities of speech—an American, a cosmopolitan (the best of America is the best cosmopolitanism) range of self-expression."[12] In some such sense, all great poetry is "language experiment." Such poetry does not leave the language unchanged but somehow extends its "boundaries," revivifies the old words, expands the limits of meaning, introduces the new and the unexpected from the old and the customary.

Whitman's interest in language was manifested in the theoretical speculation of such pieces as "Slang in America," which appeared first in the *North American Review* in November 1885, and in "An American Primer," projected lecture-notes that Whitman worked on from time to time for a number of years and which were not published until after his death (1904).[13] In both of these pieces Whitman showed an acute sense of and feel for language, and he demonstrated his awareness of the regulation of language not through externally imposed rules but through usage by the people, a "democratic" aspect that could not have failed to attract his attention. Whitman noted a relationship between the poetic impulse and the common, continual creation of slang: "Considering Language then as some mighty potentate, into the majestic audience-hall of the monarch ever enters a personage like one of Shakespere's [sic] clowns, and takes position there, and plays a part even in the stateliest ceremonies. Such is Slang, or indirection, an attempt of common humanity to escape from bald literalism, and express itself illimitably, which in highest walks produces poets and poems, and doubtless in pre-historic times gave the start to, and perfected, the whole immense tangle of the old mythologies."[14] What Whitman appears to be saying is that slang is simply one of the manifestations of the impulse to suggestiveness, an impulse which "produces poets and poems" and which produced "the old mythologies." Such an impulse springs from a desire "to escape from bald literalism"—that is, from a dissatisfaction with the merely materialistic account of the universe. In the phenomena of language growth, Whitman discovered the basic poetic impulse common to all humanity.

The Reading of Poems

When, in the 1855 Preface, Whitman said that the nation "may well go half-way to meet . . . its poets" (427) and, in "By Blue Ontario's Shore," that America "will in due time advance to meet them [her poets], there is no fear of mistake" (248), he was visualizing not a passive but an active audience participating in and indeed creating the poetic experience. Whitman's demands on the reader of poems are similar to the strenuous demands made by the modern poet (*Democratic Vistas*): "In fact, a new theory of literary composition for imaginative works of the very first class, and especially for highest poems, is the sole course open to these States. Books are to be call'd for, and supplied, on the assumption that the process of reading is not a half-sleep, but, in highest sense, an exercise, a gymnast's struggle; that the reader is to do something for himself, must be on the alert, must himself or herself construct indeed the poem, argument, history, metaphysical essay—the text furnishing the hints, the clue, the start or frame-work" (500).

But the "struggle" of the reader in his encounter with the poem is not merely an aggressive effort to understand; it is also an attempt at imaginative creation ("A Backward Glance"): "The reader will always have his or her part to do, just as much as I have had mine. I seek less to state or display any theme or thought, and more to bring you, reader, into the atmosphere of the theme or thought—there to pursue your own flight" (451). The gymnastic struggle, then, is not a mere chaotic display of brute force but an alert creativity through which the reader does indeed construct the poem. The poem comes to life only when read creatively. The poem's existence is made up of a series of such re-creations; in a very real sense it has many lives, as many lives as it has intelligent and perceptive readers.

In insisting on the creativity of the reader, Whitman was not merely displaying psychological insight (an insight that derives naturally out of his concept of idealism or eidólons and his view of the "real reality") but he was also following to its logical conclusion his doctrine of suggestiveness ("A Backward Glance"): "The word I myself put primarily for the description of them [*Leaves of Grass*] as they stand at last, is the word Suggestiveness" (451). Just as ultimate reality is inexpressible and cannot be mirrored directly, but can only be hinted at, so the reader, taking the hints given, perceives imaginatively the unknowable truth.

Poetry, Whitman insisted, does have consequences, serious consequences, and does influence the life not only of men but of a nation. One must remember, of course, that Whitman, when he wrote of poetry, had in mind primarily the great archetypal poems of the past, such as the Homeric epics and the Bible. America, too, needed its archetypal poem that at one and the same time would embody, create, and then help make prevail democratic and individualistic ideals (1855 Preface): "Of all nations the United States with veins full of poetical stuff most need poets and will doubtless have the greatest and use them the greatest" (414). Nations and peoples did, thought Whitman, make use, serious use, of poetry. But the effect of poetry is no blunderbuss effect, crudely and clumsily wrought (1855 Preface): "Without effort and without exposing in the least how it is done the greatest poet brings the spirit of any or all events and passions and scenes and persons some more and some less to bear on your individual character as you hear or read" (417).

Whitman was insistent that it was not the business of poetry to provide a cheap, immediate effect. Indeed, a sign by which inferior art was to be known was by its indulgence in the obvious tricks to achieve an unhealthy if not morbid emotional response (1855 review, "An English and an American Poet"): "It is always reserved for second-rate poems immediately to gratify. As first-rate or natural objects, in their perfect simplicity and proportion, do not startle or strike, but appear no more than matters of course, so probably natural poetry does not, for all its being the rarest, and telling of the longest and largest work."[15] The gratification of second-rate poems may be equated with sentimentality; and Whitman's abhorrence of it places him, as in so many of his attitudes, outside his Victorian era on the side of the moderns. But the effect that Whitman disparaged was not only the easy, quick emotional response; it was also the artificial effect of a self-conscious art. In one of his reviews of the 1855 edition of *Leaves of Grass* ("*Leaves of Grass*: A Volume of Poems Just Published"), Whitman said of himself: "The effects he produces in his poems are no effects of artists or the arts, but effects of the original eye or arm, or the actual atmosphere, or tree, or bird. You may feel the unconscious teaching of a fine brute, but will never feel the artificial teaching of a fine writer or speaker."[16]

Poetry does have a use, a service to perform, not only for the individual, but for the nation (*Democratic Vistas*): "Our fundamental want today in the United States . . . is of a class . . . of native authors . . .

fit to cope with our occasions, lands, permeating the whole mass of American mentality . . . affecting politics . . . and, as its grandest result, accomplishing . . . a religious and moral character beneath the political and productive and intellectual bases of the States" (457). Whitman's belief in the power of literature is almost unbounded: "Over all the arts, literature dominates, serves beyond all—shapes the character of church and school—or, at any rate, is capable of doing so. Including the literature of science, its scope is indeed unparallel'd" (459). Even such a seemingly insignificant thing as "literary style," thought Whitman, "may duly cause changes, growths, removals, greater than the longest and bloodiest war" (458).

But though the poet's accomplishments are great, such significant ends are not achieved directly or by frontal attack (1855 Preface): "The greatest poet does not moralize or make application of morals . . . he knows the soul. The soul has that measureless pride which consists in never acknowledging any lessons but its own" (417). The poet does not *tell* the reader; there is a mutual discovery of truths long submerged, a mutual creation of the genuine poetic experience. The poet has no "message" in the usual sense: "The messages of great poets to each man and woman are, Come to us on equal terms, Only then can you understand us" (418). The "lesson" of the true poet, then, is "taught" and "learned" almost unconsciously: "The attitude of great poets is to cheer up slaves and horrify despots. The turn of their necks, the sound of their feet, the motions of their wrists, are full of hazard to the one and hope to the other" (420).

The "final" effect of poetry, however, is not an end but a beginning. Although poetry achieves much, it leaves more undone (1855 Preface): "A great poem is for ages and ages in common and for all degrees and complexions and all departments and sects and for a woman as much as a man and a man as much as a woman. A great poem is no finish to a man or woman but rather a beginning" (425). Although the greatest poet may through mere attitude "cheer up slaves and horrify despots," he remains enigmatic if not silent on the deepest questions of existence (1855 review, "*Leaves of Grass*: A Volume of Poems Just Published"): "He comes to no conclusions, and does not satisfy the reader. He certainly leaves him what the serpent left the woman and the man, the taste of the Paradisiac tree of the knowledge of good and evil never to be erased again."[17] And when Whitman, like Emerson, looked about him to find his ideal poet, he found none who met his strict requirements (*Democratic Vistas*): "I feel . . . that . . . few or none have yet really spoken to this people, created a single image-making work for them, or absorb'd the central spirit and the idiosyncrasies which are theirs . . ." (474). The term Whitman substitutes for poetry, "image-making work," well suggests the creative role he demanded for readers. The poem is "image-making," a potential that cannot be realized until the proper readers submit themselves and the poem to the "gymnast's struggle."

Chapter Four
The Structure of the *Leaves*

In a critical reading of Whitman, it seems safe to make two important assumptions: the last or Deathbed Edition represented his book as he wanted it preserved, and this edition should serve as the basis for any critical estimate; Whitman's biography is largely irrelevant to his artistic achievement, and his book should be read on its own terms, not as it exemplifies or interprets his life. It should prove of some value to take a critical ramble through the whole of the last lifetime edition of *Leaves of Grass,* observing its themes, imagery, music, and catching wherever we can glimpses of its elusive structure.[1]

The moment we open the *Leaves* and glance at the first page we know that we are looking at a poetry different in kind from what went before. Whitman was the first poet in history to exploit to the full the possibilities of free verse. And there is a rare compatibility between his form and his themes; the long, unrestrained line in its free flow captures in its very form the spirit of democracy and freedom that Whitman breathed into his verses. But though Whitman's poetry represented radical departures from the past, at the same time it kept firm hold on many poetic traditions. A glance on any page of *Leaves* reveals the use of such standard devices as assonance, alliteration, repetition, inverse word order, parallelism, and many others. And though Whitman freed himself from the measured foot, his poetry is filled with a rhythm of its own, strong in the ear even if elusive to the eye. Whitman's revision of "Out of the Rocked Cradle" to "Out of the Cradle Endlessly Rocking" is indicative of his genius for instinctively achieving the inherently musical line.

The Modern Man I Sing

The cluster of poems opening *Leaves,* "Inscriptions," and the following long poem, "Starting from Paumanok," form the introductory portion of the book. These poems have their primary meaning only in relation to the poetry that follows them—for they provide a greeting to the reader and announce the themes, images, ideas, and attitudes that lie ahead. For this reason, these opening poems tend to be dependent and are rarely printed in isolation.

"Inscriptions" opens with "One's-Self I Sing," a succinct statement of the thematic heart of *Leaves,* and follows immediately with "As I Ponder'd in Silence," representing the poet's claims to the Old World muse that his poetry, like that of the past, also celebrates war—"*Waged in my book with varying fortune, with flight, advance and retreat, victory deferr'd and wavering*" (5). The suggestion is clear that *Leaves* is the modern, New World epic to serve America, as the great epics of the past served their countries. In the third poem, "In Cabin'd Ships at Sea," the poet sends his book (with its "*tones of unseen mystery*") to sea—introducing one of the major symbols of *Leaves.* Poem follows poem in "Inscriptions," some dedicating the book, some dwelling on vital themes, some glancing at the past, others peering into the future. Theme, idea, symbol, and image weave in and out, in and out, building to the fervent climax of the section with its intimate dedication to the reader.

"Starting from Paumanok" begins in autobiographical form, but it soon embraces "a soldier camp'd or carrying my knapsack and gun, or a miner in California"—a clear indication that the "I" is a composite American who embodies in some complex way the whole American (and finally, the whole *human*) experience. "Solitary, singing in the West, I strike up for a New World" is the carefree, vigorous exclamation of modern man meeting life, "what has come to the surface after so many throes and convulsions" (15), on its own terms for what it offers. The sections of "Paumanok" comprise a systematic outline of the themes of *Leaves,* and the poet summarizes:

> My comrade!
> For you to share with me two greatnesses, and a
> third one rising inclusive and more resplendent,
> The greatness of Love and Democracy, and the greatness of
> Religion.
>
> (19)

These three terms provide a key to the three major parts of *Leaves*— "Love," as it applies to the original emphasis on selfhood;

"Democracy," as it suggests the shift to national crisis; "Religion," as it identifies the final turn to spirituality. "Starting from Paumanok" appropriately concludes with an evangelistic appeal for the reader to "haste on" with the poet into the main body of the *Leaves*.

I Celebrate Myself

The first major part of *Leaves* is by far the bulkiest, extending from "Song of Myself" through "Children of Adam," "Calamus," the song section (eleven individual poems), and through the clusters "Sea-Drift" and "By the Roadside." These poems take their unity (a unity out of a wide diversity) from their overall dedication to the sketching of a New World Personality, a new conscious selfhood that provides a model for America and for modern man. This Personality may be linked to the hero of the Old Word epics, as he is meant to serve as the ideal. But herein lies the paradox. As a hero of the New World democratic society, this Personality is not placed above men but is identified with the mass as one of the common people. His glorious selfhood is no more than what is available to all mankind, but he perceives it, heightens its meaning, celebrates it—and in this lies his heroism.

This Personality is sketched forth in all its complexity of intellectual being and variety of emotional response to the world and its ways. "Song of Myself" gives birth and original shape and identity to the Personality; "Children of Adam" provides an original relationship with women; "Calamus" calls for radically new relationships with men. The eleven "songs" of what has traditionally been called the "song section" of *Leaves,* from "Salut au Monde!" through "A Song of the Rolling Earth," send the Personality forth to find his *place* on earth; the clusters from "Birds of Passage" through "By the Roadside" engage the Personality in *time* in an identification with a variety of moments in flux. Thus this first great section of *Leaves* provides the outlines of the epic hero of democracy.

"Song of Myself," "Children of Adam," and "Calamus" form the first and basic phase of the identification of the New World Personality. In "Song of Myself" the poet magnifies himself: "I celebrate myself, and sing myself, / And what I assume you shall assume, / For every atom belonging to me as good belongs to you" (25). But the self-celebration is to serve as a signal for all individuals to discover their own divine selfhood. "Song of Myself" represents an awakening of the self, a coming to consciousness for the first time of the real meaning of being alive and in the flesh, of seeing and hearing, of tasting and feeling. This awakening to consciousness penetrates beyond the senses. It dives deep within, and it soars far beyond; and it discovers secrets and uncovers mysteries—the eternity and infinity of the self, the glories of the body and soul, the completion of life through death. When at the beginning of the poem the poet says, "I, now thirty-seven years old in perfect health begin" (25), he is purposefully juxtaposing his physical birth of thirty-seven years ago with his new birth in the identification for the first time of his selfhood—a birth into a new consciousness miraculously brought about by leaning and loafing and observing a spear of summer grass.

"Children of Adam" and "Calamus" move the Personality created in "Song of Myself" from his self-imposed, imaginative isolation and provide him with lovers and comrades. The cluster "Children of Adam" sketches forth yet another ideal for the newly aware self, the ideal of the sexual innocence and pleasure of Adam and Eve before the Fall: "To the garden the world anew ascending, / Potent mates, daughters, son, preluding, / The love, the life of their bodies, meaning and being" (68). The New World Personality is to recreate the original garden in his relationship with women, and all the elements of nature are to participate in phallic and procreative celebration:

> Bridegroom night of love working surely and softly into the
>   prostrate dawn,
> Undulating into the willing and yielding day,
> Lost in the cleave of the clasping and sweet-flesh'd day.
>
> This the nucleus—after the child is born of woman, man is
>   born of woman,
> This the bath of birth, this the merge of small and large,
>   and the outlet again.
>
> (73)

As in "Song of Myself," there is a rebirth in "Children of Adam"— or simply a continuation of that reawakening begun earlier, a birth of the consciousness to new intensities of awareness, new perceptions into the meaning of human relationships. Indeed, in "Song of Myself," the poet had announced: "I am the poet of the woman the same as the man, / And I say it is as great to be a woman as to be a man, / And I

say there is nothing greater than the mother of men" (80). In claiming
to be the "poet of the woman the same as the man," Whitman was
extending his theme of equality and democratic reach to embrace difference in sex as he had extended it to embrace difference in race,
religion, and heritage. (Whitman was serious and persistent as well as
bold in his attempt to be inclusive. But what was an advanced position
for him in the nineteenth century has become a controversial position
in the twentieth. In the reference to "mother of men" in the quotation
above, some readers today will see Whitman as celebrating women's
unique biological role, while others will see his reference as one-
dimensional and patronizing.)[2]

The birth of a new consciousness in "Children of Adam" continues
into the cluster of companion poems, "Calamus," with the male re-
placing the female in the central role. In the "Calamus" poems
Whitman sketches, as counterpart of "Adam's" garden, the "paths untrodden" of ponds and calamus—another kind of innocent
Eden:

> Clear to me now standards not yet publish'd, clear to me
>   that my soul,
> That the soul of the man I speak for rejoices in comrades,
> Here by myself away from the clank of the world,
> Tallying and talk'd to here by tongues aromatic,
> No longer abash'd, (for in this secluded spot I can respond
>   as I would not dare elsewhere,)
>
> (84)

The spiritual "Calamus" attachment of man to man is to be no less
passionate and intense than the "Children of Adam" attachment—and
will, in the mass, similarly result in a new kind of society—a "continent indissoluble," "the most splendid race the sun ever shone upon,"
"divine magnetic lands" (87). Thus the spiritual comradeship of democracy fused with the sexual innocence of the Garden make up the
New World society of the freshly created Personality.

The song section of *Leaves,* following "Calamus," makes up another
loosely unified section in the book's structure and contains some of
Whitman's greatest poetry. The Personality steps forth in his newly
won identity to greet the world in "Salut au Monde!"—"What do you
see Walt Whitman? / . . . I see a great round wonder rolling through
space . . ." (101). The image of earth dominates the entire song

section, appearing and reappearing in a variety of guises, reaching a climax in the final poem, "A Song of the Rolling Earth":

> Tumbling on steadily, nothing dreading,
> Sunshine, storm, cold, heat, forever withstanding, passing,
>   carrying,
> The soul's realization and determination still inheriting,
> The fluid vacuum around and ahead still entering and dividing,
>
> . . . .
>
> The divine ship sails the divine sea.
>
> (163)

Images of place dominate the poems from "Salut au Monde!" to "A Song of the Rolling Earth." Immediately after the first poem appears "Song of the Open Road," and the Personality is launched on his journey:

> Afoot and light-hearted I take to the open road,
> Healthy, free, the world before me,
> The long brown path before me leading wherever
>   I choose.
>
> (108)

And this "long brown path" leads to "Crossing Brooklyn Ferry," in which the poet absorbs into his soul the images that identify the scene—the clouds, the sun, the people, the boat, the water.

"Song of the Answerer," "Our Old Feuillage," and "A Song of Joys" form a kind of interlude on the poet's journey over the earth: in the first, an encounter with the poet-as-Answerer; in the second, a celebration of "these compact lands tied at the hips with the belt" (124); in the last, commemoration of the joys of living—"O the joy of my soul leaning pois'd on itself, receiving identity through materials and loving them, observing characters and absorbing them" (132). The next four poems seem to roam the earth in search of the soul's joys. "Song of the Broad-Axe" asserts, "Welcome are all earth's lands, each for its kind" (135); "Song of the Exposition" commemorates a celebration of America's industrial achievement; "Song of the Redwood Tree" presents a "California song"; and "A Song for Occupations" catalogs the joys of all human activities the earth over. Throughout the entire song section, the New World Personality seems to be roaming the

earth, listening, observing, absorbing, discovering himself anew
through discovery of *place* in all its mystic complexity. He cries out in
"A Song of the Rolling Earth": "Whoever you are! motion and reflection are especially for you, / The divine ship sails the divine sea for
you" (163).

The clusters "Birds of Passage," "Sea-Drift," and "By the Roadside,"
broken by the single poem "Broadway Pageant," all together form the
final part of the first great section of *Leaves*. Throughout this section,
significantly made up in the main of clusters of short poems, the dominant image is no longer space, but time. Indeed, the titles of the
clusters—all suggesting movement, first by air, then by water, and
last on land—provide a series of images of decreasing speed: the effect
is to pass from swift movement, to a slow pace, to, finally, a full stop.
All of these images are suggestive of time, and the implication is that
the Personality (or the reader) is moved swiftly through involvement
with time, is next drifting in time, and at last is sitting silently by,
observing ("I Sit and Look Out").

"Birds of Passage" contains in some ways Whitman's most philosophical poems, dominated by the long and abstract "Song of the Universal" with its introduction of "mystic evolution" suggesting the
meaningful unfolding (or unspiralling) of time. "A Broadway Pageant"
seems in context to be merely a moment in mystic evolution, only
symbolically significant (the Japanese ambassadors visiting New York
heralding a new movement from east to west, Orient to America). In
the "Sea-Drift" poems, Whitman seems at his most hesitant and uncertain, emotionally drifting because of a failure of personal or creative
involvements. No longer taking the sweeping and spiralling philosophical view of passing events both joyous and tragic, the personally
engaged poet is too emotionally close to time to see it in terms of the
all-swallowing, all-healing mystic evolution. "Out of the Cradle Endlessly Rocking" and "As I Ebb'd with the Ocean of Life" are among
Whitman's most moving lyrics, and they portray a Personality deeply
involved in his personal entanglements. By comparison, "By the Roadside" is impersonal and disengaged, a cluster of poems of observation
and objective commentary. These transient moments of mystic evolution, miscellaneous and passing, are noted and then left by the
poet—he sees, hears, and is silent. Near the end of this cluster, the
Personality may well muse: "Locations and times—what is it in me
that meets them all, whenever and wherever, and makes me at home?"
(200).

The Throes of Democracy

The Personality given birth and identity, bodied forth on the earth and linked to mystic evolution in the first major section of *Leaves*, is, in the second section (extending from "Drum-Taps" through "Autumn Rivulets") introduced into a particular historical moment of a particular nation in crisis. In a sense, the New World hero sketched out in the abstract in the opening of *Leaves* is put to the test of war and national crisis in the succeeding pages. For the first time the poetry of *Leaves* becomes unrelievedly topical, tied to the actual happenings that shook the foundations of the nation. "Drum-Taps" is inseparably linked with the Civil War, "Memories of President Lincoln" with the death of the wartime president, and "By Blue Ontario's Shore" and "Autumn Rivulets" with America after the war as she paused on the threshold of her future and as she undertook the undramatic tasks of rehabilitation.

"Drum-Taps" comprises one of the greatest bodies of war poetry ever written. It not only introduces a new subject into the *Leaves* but represents a radical change in the mood, tone, and themes:

> No poem proud, I chanting bring to thee, nor mastery's
>   rapturous verse,
> But a cluster containing night's darkness and blood-dripping
>   wounds,
> And psalms of the dead.
>
>   (230)

But "Drum-Taps" is more than merely a miscellaneous collection of poems inspired by the war. In the first place, some unity is given to the cluster by the use of the sound image—the drum-tap—at intervals throughout, from the opening light stroke on the "stretch'd tympanum" through the "Beat! beat! drums!" to the "blow of the great convulsive drums" in the "Dirge for Two Veterans." And paralleling this dramatic variation in the drum-beat is the shifting mood and feeling of the hero—that Personality created by the earlier poems here intensely and emotionally engaged. The opening poems reflect a kind of thrill and excitement in anticipation of the adventure of war: "Mannahatta a-march—and it's O to sing it well! / It's O for a manly life in the camp" (202). But gradually this attitude shifts and the mood deepens, as the poet draws closer to the reality of war, in such poems as

"By the Bivouac's Fitful Flame"; and the emotional involvement reaches a poignant climax in the moving dramatic soliloquy for a dead comrade-soldier in "Vigil Strange I Kept on the Field One Night." In the latter part of the cluster, there is not only a rising feeling of waste and tragedy but also a detachment that embraces the misery of foe as well as friend—"For my enemy is dead, a man divine as myself is dead" (229).

This sense of national tragedy carries over from "Drum-Taps" to "Memories of President Lincoln," with its four poems dramatizing the grief of the nation at its tragic loss. "Hush'd Be the Camps To-day," "This Dust Was Once the Man," and "O Captain! My Captain!" are competently executed expressions of public sentiment on a high public occasion. But there is absent from them the deep involvement of the emotions on the personal level. Only by reducing the tragedy to the smaller compass of the individual human level was Whitman able to capture the intense and genuine feeling of the event. But as he reduced the loss to his own personal involvement in "When Lilacs Last in the Dooryard Bloom'd," at the same time he magnified the meaning of the tragedy beyond the national level by his ingenious use of symbolism, by "Lilac and star and bird twined with the chant" (239) of his soul.

The opening lines of "By Blue Ontario's Shore" suggest the nature of the major shift in emphasis in this second section of *Leaves*:

> By Blue Ontario's shore,
> As I mused of these warlike days, and of peace return'd, and
>   the dead that return no more,
> A Phantom gigantic superb, with stern visage accosted me,
> *Chant me the poem,* it said, *that comes from the soul of*
>   *America, chant me the carol of victory,*
> *And strike up the marches of Libertad, marches more*
>   *powerful yet,*
> *And sing me before you go the song of the throes of*
>   *Democracy.*
>
>   (241)

Such a confrontation of the muse in this section of *Leaves* parallels the confrontation in "Inscriptions" (where, in answer to the "Phantom," the poet asserted that his "war" was waged *For life and death, for the Body and for the eternal soul"* [6]). "By Blue Ontario's Shore" thus strikes the chord that draws the poems from "Drum-Taps" through "Autumn

Rivulets" into a unified section of *Leaves*; and, at the same time provides a long invocation (much of it mined from the 1855 Preface[3]) for American poets—"Bards of the great Idea!" (252). "Autumn Rivulets," whose long second poem, "The Return of the Heroes," sets the tone and mood of the section, is a cluster of primarily national poems, "songs of continued years" after the great struggle of the war, a miscellany as is suggested by the opening poem of the cluster, "As Consequent, Etc.": ". . . from the sea of Time, collecting vasting all, I bring, / A windrow-drift of weeds and shells" (253). These poems are the "wayward rivulets" of the nation's autumn, after the high summer passions of the Civil War; they are "waifs . . . / Wash'd on America's shores"—far more national and less personal than the "chaff, straw . . . and the sea-gluten" (185) of his earlier "Sea-Drift" poems.

The second section of *Leaves* represents in one sense the fulfillment of the prophecies of the first. The poet in the beginning had juxtaposed as the New World ideal the "simple separate person" with the "word Democratic, the word En-Masse." Individuality and the mass were emphasized throughout the early *Leaves,* with "Song of Myself" dramatizing the one and the "Calamus" vision of "companionship thick as trees" dramatizing the other. In the poems beginning with "Drum-Taps" there is a concrete realization of this ideal—the "mass" provided by the great army that arose to protect the Union; the "simple separate person" embodied idealistically in Abraham Lincoln, a man of the people who became the national leader and martyr. The national crisis of the Civil War did seem, then, a proof of the poet's confidence, a demonstration of the ability of democracy to produce both great men and great masses when the need arises.

The Way from Life to Death

The third major thematic division of *Leaves,* announced in "Proud Music of the Storm," runs through a number of individual poems and concludes with the cluster "Whispers of Heavenly Death." "Proud Music of the Storm" represents a dream vision of the poet, in which a great symphony of sounds, a blending of "hidden orchestras" and "Nature's rhythmus," enters his "lonesome slumber-chamber" and "seizes" him:

> Come forward O my soul, and let the rest retire,
> Listen, lose not, it is toward thee they tend,

> Parting the midnight, entering my slumber-chamber,
> For thee they sing and dance O soul.
>
> (283)

From the extraordinary parade of sights and sounds originating the world around, the poet awakes with "the clew" he had long sought:

> Haply what thou hast heard O soul was not the sounds of winds,
> Nor dream of raging storm, nor sea-hawk's flapping wings
>   nor harsh scream,
>
> . . . .
>
> But to a new rhythmus fitted for thee,
> Poems bridging the way from Life to Death, vaguely wafted
>   in night air, uncaught, unwritten,
> Which let us go forth in the bold day and write.
>
> (287)

Like the Phantom of "Inscriptions" and "By Blue Ontario's Shore," the storm-music provides the poet's soul with a "new rhythmus," the theme of death and its meaning in a context of life.

"Passage to India," "Prayer of Columbus," "The Sleepers," "To Think of Time," and the cluster "Whispers of Heavenly Death," all are poems "bridging the way from Life to Death." "Passage to India" is one of Whitman's most ecstatic poems, in which the poet notes the remarkable feats of engineers in physically rounding the globe and then calls for a parallel spiritual achievement. In his spiritual venturing and daring, the poet seems to peer into eternity as he experiences a foretaste of death:

> O soul thou pleasest me, I thee,
> Sailing these seas or on the hills, or waking in the night,
> Thoughts, silent thoughts, of Time and Space and Death,
>   like waters flowing,
> Bear me indeed as through the regions infinite,
> Whose air I breath, whose ripples hear, lave me all over,
> Bathe me O God in thee, mounting to thee,
> I and my soul to range in range of thee.
>
> (293)

Similarly, "Prayer of Columbus" presents insight into the spiritual significance of death, as the old, feeble, destitute and ridiculed Columbus turns to the "ray of light, steady, ineffable . . . / Light rare untellable, lighting the very light" in prayer, and glimpses the bridge "from Life to Death":

> As if some miracle, some hand divine unseal'd my eyes,
> Shadowy vast shapes smile through the air and sky,
> And on the distant waves sail countless ships,
> And anthems in new tongues I hear saluting me.
>
> (296)

Whitman's dream-poem, "The Sleepers," derives much of its symbolic meaning from its placement in this thematic grouping of poems. The poet wanders all night in his vision—"confused, lost to myself, ill-assorted, contradictory, / Pausing, gazing, bending, and stopping" (297). But before the vision is completed, it becomes clear that the experience is symbolic. The night that "pervades" and "infolds" the wretched and the sick, the insane and the dying, as well as the living and loving, represents the world of spirituality, tending always toward an all-encompassing unity; while the day represents the world of physical being and existence. At the end of the poem, as the poet awakens from his dream, he says of the night:

> I love the rich running day, but I do not desert her in
>   whom I lay so long,
> I know not how I came of you and I know not where I go
>   with you, but I know I came well and shall go well.
>
> (303)

As "The Sleepers" bridges the "way from Life to Death" through the symbolic drama of dreams, "To Think of Time" provides a bridge by direct contemplation of death—"To think the thought of death merged in the thought of materials" (304). The poem is one long meditation on the intuitive assurance of eternity, concluding with a defiant affirmation:

> I swear I think there is nothing but immortality!
> That the exquisite scheme is for it, and the nebulous float

is for it, and the cohering is for it!
And all preparation is for it—and identity is for it—and life
    and materials altogether for it!

(308)

A number of brief "bridges" are brought together in the cluster
"Whispers of Heavenly Death," in which the "labial gossip of night"
transfigures death into "Some parturition rather, some solemn immortal birth" (309). At the beginning of the cluster the poet challenges
his soul to "Walk out with me toward the unknown region"; and he
images the sensation of death:

Then we burst forth, we float,
In Time and Space O soul, prepared for them,
Equal, equipt at last, (O joy! O fruit of all!) them to fulfil
    O soul.

(309)

The dominant poem of the group is "Chanting the Square Deific," a
sketch of the archetypal patterns of all religious myth—the Jehovah,
the Consolator, the Satan, and the Santa Spirita—the "general soul"
(311) that finishes the square. Clearly the Santa Spirita is the unifying
principle of the universe that provides a bridge from life to death. Near
the end of the cluster, the poet makes "The Last Invocation": "Let me
glide noiselessly forth; / With the key of softness unlock the locks—
with a whisper, / Set ope the doors O soul" (316).

Special Songs Before I Go

With "Whispers of Heavenly Death" Whitman draws the main body
of his *Leaves* to a close. The rest is farewell. He addresses America
at the beginning of "Thou Mother with Thy Equal Brood": "Thou
varied chain of different States, yet one identity only, / A special song
before I go I'd sing o'er all the rest, / For thee, the future" (317).
In this last major review of his New World themes, the poet looks
to "Time's spirals rounding" (320) for the real fulfillment of the
democratic promise. "From Noon to Starry Night" provides a cluster

of miscellaneous poems that play variations on all his themes, a recapitulation of the main moods and feelings of the *Leaves*. The section opens with a call by the poet on "Thou Orb Aloft Full-Dazzling," the "hot October noon," to: "Prepare the later afternoon of me myself—prepare my lengthening shadows, / Prepare my starry nights" (322). And the cluster closes with a retrospective view in "A Clear Midnight":

> This is thy hour O soul, thy free flight into the wordless,
> Away from books, away from art, the day erased, the
>   lesson done,
> Thee fully forth emerging, silent, gazing, pondering the
>   themes thou lovest best,
> Night, sleep, death and the stars.
>
>   (338)

And with this meditation, the poet is prepared for his final farewell in "Songs of Parting." Corresponding in nature and function to "Inscriptions" at the beginning, this last cluster contains a similar note of fervency and evangelistic appeal: "O book, O chants! must all then amount to but this? / Must we barely arrive at this beginning of us?— and yet it is enough, O soul" (339). All of the poems deal, directly or indirectly, with death; and, near the end (as in "Inscriptions"), a number of brief poems establish an intimacy between reader and poet, as he bids goodbye. The cluster then ends with "So Long!": "To conclude, I announce what comes after me" (348). This prophecy outlines a fulfillment of all the *Leaves* have called for, a final achievement of the New World Personality and the democratic ideal. And the poet ends: "Remember my words, I may again return, / I love you, I depart from materials, / I am as one disembodied, triumphant, dead" (350). So the poet departs, his poem done. The annexes that follow are just that— additions essentially superfluous to the main structure. Though "Sands at Seventy," "Good-bye My Fancy," and "Old Age Echoes" contain some vivid and vigorous poems, they are simply what their titles indicate, miscellanies left over after the main business—the building of the *Leaves*—was concluded.

A recapitulation of the structure of *Leaves* suggests the emotional logic in the ordering of its parts:

Introductory: The Modern Man I Sing
  Inscriptions
  "Starting from Paumanok"

1. I Celebrate Myself
  "Song of Myself"
  Children of Adam   }   identity and relations
  Calamus

  Songs (eleven poems)   }   space: the earth

  Birds of Passage
  "A Broadway Pageant"   }   time: mystic evolution
  Sea-Drift
  By the Roadside

2. The Throes of Democracy
  Drum-Taps   }   crisis
  Memories of President Lincoln

  "By Blue Ontario's Shore"   }   continued years
  Autumn Rivulets

3. The Way from Life to Death
  "Proud Music of the Storm"
  "Passage to India"
  "Prayer of Columbus"
  "The Sleepers"
  "To Think of Time"
  Whispers of Heavenly Death

Concluding: Special Songs Before I Go
  "Thou Mother with Thy Equal Brood"
  From Noon to Starry Night
  Songs of Parting

Afterthoughts: The Annexes
  Sands at Seventy
  Good-Bye My Fancy
  Old Age Echoes

  In effect the structure of *Leaves* is pyramidal, a metaphor that seems
especially apt when the comparative bulk of the three basic parts is

taken into account. Part 1 is a bit over twice the length of part 2, part 2 double the size of part 3:

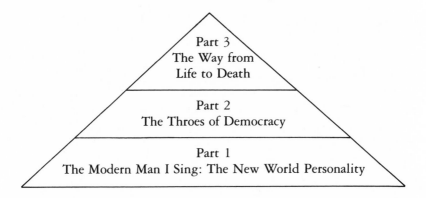

The pyramid not only suggests the relative dependence of the various parts—the Personality must be created before he can be engaged in a particular time and place, and his being and existence and engagement must precede his envelopment in the world of spirituality—but it suggests, too, the proportionate preoccupations of Modern Man: mostly personal and involved with identity of self in life, but maturely concerned for the society and the state, and with profound moments of spiritual meditation on the bridges leading from Life to Death.

Chapter Five

The Individual Leaves

Whitman arranged all his poems in *Leaves of Grass* so as to provide them with contexts in depth. As a result, any one of his poems read out of the *Leaves* is diminished somewhat in meaning—the meaning provided by the entire thematic and emotional structure of *Leaves*. Nevertheless, many of his poems stand alone, in solitude, with admirable independence. And they deserve the close attention that criticism can best make of poems in isolation.

Critical opinion and popular opinion are not divided in the case of Whitman. The best liked poems are usually those that are acclaimed by the critics. And most lists of Whitman's finest poems show a great deal of agreement. At the top and placed in a unique position, not only in Whitman's work but in the whole literary tradition, is "Song of Myself." Next appears a group of four poems that can rank with the greatest poetry of Whitman's or almost any other century: "Crossing Brooklyn Ferry," "Out of the Cradle Endlessly Rocking," "When Lilacs Last in the Dooryard Bloom'd," and "Passage to India." Four additional poems make up a second group somewhat different in kind from the first: "Song of the Open Road," "Song of the Broad-Axe," "By Blue Ontario's Shore," and "The Sleepers." Finally, in a separate category by themselves are a number of briefer lyrics, sometimes brilliant, sometimes profound—such poems as "One's-Self I Sing," "I Hear America Singing," "When I Heard the Learn'd Astronomer," "The Dalliance of the Eagles," "Sparkles from the Wheel," "Vigil Strange I Kept on the Field One Night," "Prayer of Columbus," "A Noiseless Patient Spider."[1]

"Song of Myself"

By any standards "Song of Myself" is one of the great long poems in the language. Its very length, however, has sometimes worked against its popularity, particularly as it seemed to lack coherence and direction. But it is now generally agreed that "Song of Myself" has a structure, and that there is in it some kind of progression, not aimless wandering. Although there is no critical unanimity as to what the structure is, there is surprising agreement as to the validity of grouping the fifty-two sections of the poem under a number of major headings.[2]

In addition to some kind of structure, the critics are agreed that a major ingredient of the poem is some kind of mysticism[3]—or something so like mysticism that the terms of the mystic are of value in any discussion. It is, indeed, useful to view the poem through the framework of the traditional mystical experience, as sketched forth briefly in William James's *Varieties of Religious Experience* and, more particularly, as set forth in detail in Evelyn Underhill's *Mysticism: A Study in the Nature and Development of Man's Spiritual Consciousness.*[4]

When viewed in terms of the phases of the traditional mystical experience, "Song of Myself" takes on a comprehensive structural shape:

Sections 1–5: Entry into the mystical state

Sections 6–16: Awakening of self

Sections 17–32: Purification of self (but by glorifying, not mortifying, the senses)

Sections 33–37: Illumination and the dark night of the soul

Sections 38–43: Union (emphasis on faith and love)

Sections 44–49: Union (emphasis on perception)

Sections 50–52: Emergence from mystical state

The progression of the poet through these states is demonstrable by close examination of the poem.[5] But there is a major and perhaps crucial difference between the poet's and the traditional experience. The traditional mystic attempted to annihilate himself and mortify his senses in preparation for absorption into the Transcendent. Whitman magnifies the self and glorifies the senses in his progress toward Union.

Sections 1–5: *Entry into the mystical state*   By leaning, loafing and inviting his soul, and by "observing a spear of summer grass" (25), the poet precipitates the mystical trance. In these opening sections he rids himself of all human-associated things and goes to the woods, "undisguised and naked," where he will "permit to speak at every hazard, / Nature without check with original energy" (25). In section 5 the soul becomes intimate with the poet ("you settled your head athwart my hips and gently turn'd over upon me" [28]) and infuses him

with spirituality, transfiguring him and endowing him with a higher
perception: "Swiftly arose and spread around me the peace and knowledge that pass all the argument of the earth" (28). The poet is launched
on his mystical journey.

   Sections 6–16: *Awakening of self*   Traditionally the mystic ad-
vances on the Way by first awakening to other and higher levels of
consciousness. The poet in these sections is involved in a continually
expanding view of the self: he extends his identification of self further
and further until it seems to embrace all mankind. He exclaims in
section 13:

> In me the caresser of life wherever moving, backward as
>   well as forward sluing,
> To niches aside and junior bending, not a person or
>   object missing,
> Absorbing all to myself and for this song.
>
>   (32)

This expanding identification reaches a climax in the long catalog of
section 15, so that the poet may cry out in section 16, "Of every hue
and caste am I, of every rank and religion" (36).

   Sections 17–32: *Purification of self*   In section 17 the poet seems
to pause and reflect: "These are really the thoughts of all men in all
ages and lands, they are not original with me" (37). They are aimed at
the "untying of the riddle"—mystic knowledge of the self and the
universe. In these sections the poet turns from the vast extension of his
identity to the pervasive equality of all being (section 19): "This is the
meal equally set, this the meat for natural hunger" (37). This theme
leads to the claim (section 21): "I am the poet of the Body and I am
the poet of the Soul" (39). Gradually the poet works his way to the
main point of these sections (section 24): "Voices indecent by me clar-
ified and transfigur'd" (42). This prophecy is fulfilled in the brilliant
passage on touch (sections 28–30), in which sexual ecstasy and fulfillment lead to a "new identity," granting a deeper perception. Thus the
poet inverts the traditional mystical pattern: he purifies the senses not
by mortification but by transfiguration and glorification.

Sections 33–37: *Illumination and the dark night of the soul* Section 33 begins by announcing a new and higher stage of perception: "Space and Time! now I see it is true, what I guess'd at, / What I guess'd when I loaf'd on the grass" (48). Like the traditional mystic, the poet has won his way through purification to illumination, in which he achieves glimpses of the mystic knowledge he strives for. The poet is freed from life's physical restraints and momentarily transcends space and time: "My ties and ballasts leave me, my elbows rest in seagaps / . . . I am afoot with my vision" (48). The poet soars like a meteor in his new-won insight: "Speeding through space, speeding through heaven and the stars" (50). But gradually, and still in section 33, the mood shifts from exhilaration and exultation to darkness and even despair: "Agonies are one of my changes of garments, / I do not ask the wounded person how he feels, I myself become the wounded person" (52). This "dark night of the Soul," a massive identification with the sick and the injured, the destitute and the rejected, the unwanted and the despised, intensifies through the wartime massacre of section 34 and the sea-battle tragedy of sections 35 and 36, culminating in section 37: "Askers embody themselves in me and I am embodied in them, / I project my hat, sit shame-faced, and beg" (56).

Sections 38–43: *Union (emphasis on faith and love)* Section 38 opens with an abrupt shift in attitude:

> Enough! enough! enough!
> Somehow I have been stunn'd. Stand back!
> Give me a little time beyond my cuff'd head, slumbers,
>   dreams, gaping,
> I discover myself on the verge of a usual mistake.
>
> (56)

There follows through several sections the Christ identification: "That I could look with a separate look on my own crucifixion and bloody crowning! . . . / Corpses rise, gashes heal, fastenings roll from me" (56). The poet has achieved sudden knowledge, like the knowledge of the miraculously risen Christ—absolute mystic knowledge, the knowledge of Union that bestows divine energy and certainty: "I troop forth replenish'd with supreme power, one of an average unending procession" (56). For the remainder of these sections the poet speeds about the earth, "bringing help for the sick as they pant on their backs" (58) and bolstering the faith of the "Down-hearted doubters dull and excluded" (61).

Sections 44–49: *Union (emphasis on perception)*   Section 44 opens with a change of direction: "It is time to explain myself—let us stand up" (61). In these sections the poet's "supreme power" becomes the power of mystic insight, insight into the fundamental questions of existence. Time (section 44): "The clock indicates the moment—but what does eternity indicate?" (61). Space (section 45): "I open my scuttle at night and see the far-sprinkled systems" (63). These thoughts and observations lead to the intuitive certainty (section 46): "I know I have the best of time and space, and was never measured and never will be measured" (63). Sections 46 and 47 charge each man to travel his own journey—"I have no chair, no church, no philosophy" (64); "I teach straying from me" (65). The poet contemplates God (section 48): "I hear and behold God in every object, yet understand God not in the least" (66). And death (section 49): "And as to you Death, and you bitter hug of mortality, it is idle to try to alarm me" (66). Throughout these sections the poet repeatedly *knows;* but, unable to explain his knowledge intellectually, he can only chant his assurance in rhapsodic and vivid terms.

Sections 50–52: *Emergence from mystical state*   Paralleling the opening sections, these concluding sections portray the poet emerging from his mystical trance: "Wrench'd and sweaty—calm and cool then my body becomes, / I sleep—I sleep long" (67). Exhausted both physically and spiritually by his mystical experience, the poet first falls into a deep sleep, and then gropes his way back to consciousness of the ordinary world, unable to embody the meaning of what he has learned in language: "I do not know it—it is without name—it is a word unsaid, / It is not in any dictionary, utterance, symbol" (67). He can only hint at the significance: "It is not chaos or death—it is form, union, plan—it is eternal life—it is Happiness" (67). The last sections comprise the poet's final farewell and testament: "I bequeath myself to the dirt to grow from the grass I love, / If you want me again look for me under your boot-soles" (68). The reader can rediscover the poet by observing his own spear of summer grass and by launching his own mystical journey.

The question is frequently raised as to whether Whitman ever had a real mystical experience, and whether "Song of Myself" is "valid." It is, poetically, an irrelevant question. The poem may be accepted as a *dramatization,* not a transcription of an actual experience. Whitman's imagination was sufficiently vigorous and expansive to embrace the experience and embody it in his own terms. What fired Whitman's imagination were probably the fragments of many experiences, semi-mystical and transcendent, that he transfigured into the magic of poetry. In the Illumination opening section 33, what he sees as true is what he had guessed at when he "loaf'd on the grass," "lay alone," in his bed, or as he "walk'd the beach under the paling stars of the morning" (48). Perhaps Whitman permits a glimpse here of the varied experiences from which his imagination fused the single experience of the poem. But though the poem is drama, it is not less valid or authentic than Milton's *Paradise Lost* or Eliot's *Waste Land.* Like them, "Song of Myself" has the only kind of validity that counts—the poetic validity of imaginative integrity and truth.

"Ferry," "Cradle," "Lilac," and "India"

There is general critical agreement that, aside from "Song of Myself," Whitman's greatest poems are "Crossing Brooklyn Ferry" (1856), "Out of the Cradle Endlessly Rocking" (1860), "When Lilacs Last in the Dooryard Bloom'd" (1865), and "Passage to India" (1871). These four poems not only are Whitman's best but also represent the several individual creative periods of his poetic career. A brief examination of them in sequence not only reveals Whitman at the height of his powers but also indicates his characteristic themes and attitudes.

"Crossing Brooklyn Ferry" dramatizes a simple, ordinary experience in such a way as to symbolize the mystic unity that pervades all mankind and the universe. The crossing on the ferry by its very nature brings together in time many diverse people, holds them together in unity, lifts them for a moment beyond the reach of space and time, then disperses them. The poet sees in this moment of transcendence, when the ferry crowds are held suspended on the water between the shores, a symbol of the human fate and destiny: "The simple, compact, well-join'd scheme, myself disintegrated, every one disintegrated yet part of the scheme" (116). When the poet cries out at the opening of section 3, "It avails not, time nor place—distance avails not" (116), he indicates the dramatic movement of the poem: the poet will fuse himself with the reader in order to persuade him of the universal identity.

All the images of the ferry-scene are invoked in catalog to assist in the approaching identity. And then the poet pauses again in section 5 and asks: "What is it then between us? / What is the count of the scores or hundreds of years between us? / Whatever it is, it avails not—distance avails not, and place avails not" (118). He next turns to the intimate emotional relationships that fuse him with the reader, and he asserts: "I too had been struck from the float forever held in solution" (118)—a chemical figure of a solid precipitated from a liquid (the individual soul "precipitated" from the oversoul or universal spirit). The poet (like the reader) had been touched by the "dark patches," had known "what it was to be evil" (118).

In section 7 the climax seems near as the poet cries out, "Closer yet I approach you," and slyly (and disconcertingly) suggests, "Who knows, for all the distance, but I am as good as looking at you now, for all you cannot see me?" (119). And the climax is reached in section 8, as the poet works his way into the very being of the reader:

> What is more subtle than this which ties me to the woman
>   or man that looks in my face?
> Which fuses me into you now, and pours my meaning into
>   you?
>
>   (119)

Immediately after this direct identification, the poet assumes his task accomplished—"We understand then do we not?" The remainder of the poem is devoted to a kind of ritualistic verbal dance reinvoking all of the images of the poem that assisted the poet in fusing with the reader—the "dumb, beautiful ministers" that have furnished their "parts toward the soul" (120).

While "Crossing Brooklyn Ferry" might be called Whitman's public love poem, directed at everybody, and most intimately at the reader, "Out of the Cradle Endlessly Rocking" is a private love poem, directed not outward but inward, in on itself and the poet's soul. "Out of the Cradle" is also heavily symbolic, removed from the immediacy of "Ferry" by projection backward in time to a boy's experience, and outward in space to the birds' love drama. It is a "reminiscence" of the crucial semimystic experience that made a poet out of a boy and gave him a central theme. The whole effect of the opening lines is by their very frenzy to sweep the reader into the experience of overwhelming memory that takes possession of the poet and carries him back—"by these tears a little boy again, / Throwing myself on the sand, confronting the waves" (180).

The "curious boy, . . . / Cautiously peering, absorbing, translating," first hears the love carol of the happy birds as they bask in their nest together: "*Shine! shine! shine! / Pour down your warmth, great sun!*" (180). But after the she-bird disappears, "may-be killed," the he-bird begins his song of longing, a sad carol of the night: "*Carols of lonesome love! death's carols! / Carols under that lagging, yellow, waning moon!*" (182). The listening boy becomes ecstatic as his ears "swiftly" deposit the "aria's meaning" into his soul, and a colloquy begins among a "trio"—the bird, the sea, and the boy's soul—a colloquy directed at the boy as "outsetting bard" (183).

In the rhapsodic soliloquy of his soul, the boy recognizes the origin of poetic inspiration—"A thousand warbling echoes have started to life within me, never to die" (183)—and makes a direct identification with the bird: "O you singer solitary, singing by yourself, projecting me" (184). Although the boy's soul takes as its own the theme of "unsatisfied love," the "sweet hell within," there seems still to be something lacking: "O give me the clew! (it lurks in the night here somewhere)" (184). In answer to this plea, the sea responds from its "liquid rims and wet sands," "hissing melodious" the "delicious word death." The boy's ecstasy reaches its climax: "Creeping thence steadily up to my ears and laving me softly all over, / Death, death, death, death, death" (184).

The boy "fuses" the song of his "dusky demon and brother" with the "thousand responsive songs" of his soul, and adds to them "the key, the word up from the waves." As the outsetting bard he has discovered the "clew" to his themes, given him by the sea: "(Or like some old crone rocking the cradle, swathed in sweet garments, bending aside,) / The sea whisper'd me" (184). The poem thus ends, as it begins ("Out of the cradle endlessly rocking"), with the sea represented by the metaphor of birth: the "delicious word," as the boy has intuitively apprehended in the ecstasy of his soul, is the "clew" to life, the "key" to rebirth and eternity. "Lonesome love" is transfigured by it into imaginative and spiritual fulfillment.

Like "Out of the Cradle," "When Lilacs Last in the Dooryard Bloom'd" is concerned with love and death, but of a different kind and on a different level. The poem opens, like the traditional elegy, with an expression of uncontrollable grief—"O powerful western

fallen star! / O shades of night—O moody, tearful night!" (233).
By the time the poem concludes, the grief has subsided and the lines
are filled with the mood of reconciliation. The drama of the poem
lies in the narrative of the poet's vacillation between the lilacs and
the hermit-thrush, between the overpowering emotion of loving grief
for the dead president and the subdued emotion brought by insight
into the spiritual meaning of death. The structure of the poem is
cyclic in nature, moving from star to lilac to bird, and back to star
again, to repeat the circle—but eventually settling with the hermit-
thrush.

The emotions of the poem are embodied in a number of powerful
symbols. The western star is Abraham Lincoln, its fixed position in
the heavens suggesting his steady leadership of the nation. The "harsh
surrounding cloud" represents death and the tragic loss it leaves in its
wake. The lilacs, returning every spring, symbolize the eternal memory of the president and the strong love of the poet for him. The hermit-thrush represents the voice of spirituality, his song "Death's outlet
song of life" (232).

When the poet, his emotions spent, finally heeds the call of the
hermit-thrush, it is to follow him to the swamp cedars with two "com-
panions": the "thought of death" (memory of Lincoln) and the "sacred
knowledge of death" (spiritual insight). There by the "shores of the
water," on the "path by the swamp in the dimness," he hears the
thrush's carol of death, a carol of joy and praise for the "*dark mother*"
and "*strong deliveress*" (237). With his soul "tallying" the bird's song,
the poet has a moment of spiritual ecstasy that bestows a vision con-
firming the bird's joy in death. With this insight the poet becomes
reconciled to death, and his grief subsides. The closing section of the
poem ritualistically chants the poet's gentle and gradual release from
the powerful grip of his emotions, concluding: "Lilac and star and bird
twined with the chant of my soul, / There in the fragrant pines and
the cedars dusk and dim" (239).

"Passage to India," though not directly concerned with death as are
"Out of the Cradle" and "When Lilacs Last," is closely related to these
poems and "Crossing Brooklyn Ferry" in its dominant theme of spirituality. As the point of departure of his poem Whitman celebrates the
rounding of the globe achieved by the great works of engineers—the
Suez Canal, the transoceanic cable, and the transcontinental railroad.
What fired his poetic imagination was that on California's shores
man looked west not to new lands, but back to the beginning, to

civilization's cradle, to the land of "budding bibles," to man's physical and spiritual origins—all symbolized by India.

The theme of the poem is not materialistic achievement, however, but spiritual fusion. Whitman calls for an achievement of the soul to match the marvelous achievement of the hands. The main substance of the poem is made up of the poet's sweeping visions. The first is spatial, climaxed by the "tableaus twain" of section 3 that dramatize crossing through the canal and traveling over the railroad. The second is temporal, a view of time as it has been embodied sequentially in myth (section 5) and as it has been set forth in history (section 6). In the latter is imbedded a vivid vignette of Columbus, who himself had, like the poet, dreamed of a passage to India.

As the poet calls out in section 7 for passage to "primal thought," to "reason's early paradise, / Back, back to wisdom's birth, to innocent intuitions" (292), his desire approaches that of the mystic to transcend time and space and to merge with the Transcendent. Section 8 is a dramatization of that merging as only the poet can portray it in the ecstasy of his vision: "Bathe me O God in thee, mounting to thee, / I and my soul to range in range of thee" (293). This mystical merge which can be sensed in life is but a foretaste of the Union attained in death. For when the time is "achiev'd," "The seas all cross'd, weather'd the capes, the voyage done," and the soul "frontest God"—"As fill'd with friendship, love complete, and Elder Brother found, / The Younger melts in fondness in his arms" (293). The final section of the poem is a fervent appeal by the poet to his soul to sail out, to "steer for the deep waters only" (294)—to achieve that spiritual union for which the rounding of the globe has been but preparation.

"Open Road," "Broad-Axe," "Ontario's Shore," and "Sleepers"

A second group of poems, not necessarily inferior to the first (but without their wide, popular appeal) would appear high on the lists of most critics. "Song of the Open Road" (1856), "Song of the Broad-Axe" (1856), "By Blue Ontario's Shore" (1856), and "The Sleepers" (1855), though they were originally composed at about the same time, are astonishingly varied in theme and imagery. "Song of the Open Road" supplies the basic image of Whitman's vagabond poet; "Song of the Broad-Axe" unites in one symbol the varied and diverse progression of man in mystic evolution; "By Blue Ontario's Shore" sketches an archetypal poet to sing America and democracy; and "The Sleepers" delves deeply into man's psyche by dramatizing his dreams. Each of these poems, by its singularity in theme and subject, adds an individual dimension to Whitman's achievement.

"Song of the Open Road" begins with the image of the poet striding joyously down the roadways of the country:

> Afoot and light-hearted I take to the open road,
> Healthy, free, the world before me,
> The long brown path before me leading wherever
>   I choose.
>
> (108)

On this initial visual image of the vagabond wandering the earth, carefree and happy, Whitman starts adding layer after layer of meaning. The poem celebrates two aspects of the vagabond's life: (1) the wandering, the sheer joy of movement and diversity of experience; (2) the direct involvement with nature in the innocence and validity of its *naturalness,* its original and uncorrupted form.

The poet has not gone very far before it becomes clear that his journey is symbolic. "Done with indoor complaints, libraries, querulous criticisms, / Strong and content I travel the open road" (108). The poet is disavowing one way of life and embracing another. The "open road" becomes the symbol of the new way, of a fresh and joyous way of encountering experience whatever it brings, of stepping forth free of custom and tradition and living life fully in accord with instinct and intuitive insight: "From this hour I ordain myself loos'd of limits and imaginary lines, / Going where I list, my own master total and absolute" (109). In effect, to travel the open road is to assert spiritual independence and self-reliance, to realize divine selfhood: "Now I see the secret of the making of the best persons, / It is to grow in the open air and to eat and sleep with the earth" (110). Each man must discover his individual—and original—relation with the universe.

Beginning in section 9 ("Allons! whoever you are come travel with me!" [111]), the poet launches a personal appeal to the reader that forms the dramatic structure of the last seven sections of the poem, an appeal that recurs and gradually intensifies to a peak of frenzy and fervor. Emphasis is placed on moving, on going, on arising and traveling: "Allons! we must not stop here, / However sweet these laid-up stores, however convenient this dwelling we cannot remain here"

(112). A rejection of the static and the materialistic, the appeal is an affirmation of the joy of transience, of the movement through time in appointed cycles: "Journeyers over consecutive seasons, over the years, the curious years each emerging from that which preceded it" (113). The poet celebrates the living world of continual change over the stagnant world of *things* in stasis (compare John Keats's "Ode on a Grecian Urn," and the appeal of the static world depicted in the marble scene on the urn). The spiritual life is not the static life, but the life on the open road, "the procession of souls along the grand roads of the universe" (114).

The poet's appeal to the reader is an appeal to involvement in all the diversity and hardships of the individualized life: "My call is the call of battle, I nourish active rebellion" (115). And he concludes by extending his hand with a personal invitation that has an evangelistic ring: "Camerado, I give you my hand! / I give you my love more precious than money, / . . . Will you give me your self? will you come travel with me? / Shall we stick by each other as long as we live?" (115).

Unlike "Song of the Open Road," "Song of the Broad-Axe" takes as its central symbol a material object—the tool of the pioneer. The axe is introduced vividly ("Weapon shapely, naked, wan" [135]), and it then is used as a nucleus around which to cluster innumerable and varied images: "Strong shapes and attributes of strong shapes, masculine trades, sights and sounds, / Long varied train of an emblem, dabs of music" (135). With this suggestion of the poem's structure, Whitman proceeds to pile image on image, the axe serving to symbolize the unity pervading a limitless diversity.

"Welcome are all earth's lands, each for its kind," the poet begins—including the "lands of the manly and rugged ores" (134) from which the axe came. In section 3 the poet catalogs a multitude of builders of all places and times for whom their instrument, whether creative or destructive, was vital. "The butcher in the slaughter-house," "the house-builder at work," "spar-makers in the spar-yard," "the city fireman," "the primal patient mechanics, the architects and engineers," "the Roman lictors preceding the consuls, / The antique European warrior with his axe in combat"—the emphasis is placed on the men, not on structures and things, on "The limber motion of brawny young arms and hips in easy costumes" (136–37). The most important creation of the axe (or of any tool) is not the *thing* it makes but the man who wields it—"nothing endures but personal qualities" (138).

The axe thus comes to symbolize Man in the creative role of shaping himself and his life. Greatness can never reside in things, only in people: "A great city is that which has the greatest men and women, / If it be a few ragged huts it is still the greatest city in the whole world" (138). The pomp of material show is as nothing before the individual who has fully realized his selfhood: "How beggarly appear arguments before a defiant deed! / How the floridness of the materials of cities shrivels before a man's or woman's look!" (139).

Beginning in the precise middle of the poem, with section 7, the poet launches a survey of the axe's role in the history of civilization. It "served the fluent-tongued and subtle-sensed Greek, and long ere the Greek" (139). The European headsman "stands mask'd, clothed in red, with huge legs and strong naked arms, / And leans on a ponderous axe" (140). In section 9, the "axe leaps" to America: "The solid forest gives fluid utterances, / They tumble forth, they rise and form" (140). Using the refrain, "The shapes arise!" the poet catalogs all the diverse structures of America, "factories, arsenals, foundries, markets" (141), coffins, beds, cradles, homes, "shapes of doors giving many exits and entrances" (142). All these diverse shapes make up the shape of Democracy, "silent," "possess'd of herself." And the poem closes projecting the shapes of the future, "shapes of Democracy total," "shapes bracing the earth and braced with the whole earth" (142). The axe comes finally to symbolize the totality of mankind fulfilling its destiny in mystic evolution.

"By Blue Ontario's Shore" embodies much of the 1855 Preface, for many lines of the prose are placed in the poem without change. Whitman's revisions of the poem, together with his placement of it after "Drum-Taps" and "Memories of President Lincoln" in Leaves, suggest that he could most validly relate the mood, tone, and meaning of the 1855 Preface to the 1865 conclusion of the Civil War—that crucial event which symbolized the coming of age of the nation. To prevent his poem from becoming mere polemic and exhortation, Whitman invented a dramatic framework to give it structure and direction. As he sits musing on the Civil War beside "blue Ontario's shore," he is accosted by "a Phantom gigantic superb, with stern visage" (241). This New World muse calls on the poet to chant a "carol of victory," to sing the song of "the throes of Democracy" (241).

Whitman willingly undertakes the task—speaking for "A Nation announcing itself" (241). The proof of the nation is "in time and deeds": "We are executive in ourselves, we are sufficient in the variety of ourselves" (241). America, in preserving the Union, has put its national selfhood to the supreme test—and endured. The central principle of Democracy lies not in things but within individuals: "Produce great Persons, the rest follows" (242). The poet's carol will not be sung in dulcet tones of "piety and conformity": "I am he who tauntingly compels men, women, nations, / Crying, Leap from your seats and contend for your lives!" (242). Like the self-reliant individual, America "stands removed, spacious, composite, sound, initiates the true use of precedents" (242).

In section 9, the poet again hears the voice of the Phantom, "arising demanding bards": "By them all native and grand, by them alone can these States be fused into the compact organism of a Nation" (245). Here Whitman expands on this favorite theme, setting forth the qualifications of the New World poet of Democracy: "He is the arbiter of the diverse, he is the key, / He is the equalizer of his age and land" (245). The American bard will hold a commanding position in society: "For the great Idea, the idea of perfect and free individuals, / For that, the bard walks in advance, leader of leaders" (246).

The poet's celebration of America, however, is to be simply another form of the celebration of Self: "It is not the earth, it is not America who is so great, / It is I who am great or to be great, it is You up there, or any one" (249). For America is no more than the people themselves: "O I see flashing that this America is only you and me" (250). The poet thus symbolically becomes the nation, and magnifies himself to embrace it all: "Copious as you are I absorb you all in myself, and become the master myself" (251).

As the poem draws to a close, the poet, "thrill'd with the power's pulsations," is granted a vision: "And I saw the free souls of poets, / The loftiest bards of past ages strode before me" (251). Taken aback by this parade of past poets when he had just called for new bards, the poet cries out: "O my rapt verse, my call, mock me not! / Not for the bards of the past, not to invoke them have I launch'd you forth" (252). And he calls out: "Bards for my own land only I invoke," "Bards of the great Idea!" (252). This concluding drama of a discordant vision serves as a vivid reminder that "By Blue Ontario's Shore" is a poem not of the present condition but of the vistas of the future; it is less reality than a prophecy.

All of "The Sleepers" is a vision, a penetration by the poet into the remarkable world of dreams. In this symbolic drama of "Sleep-Chasings" (a former title), the poet seems to anticipate the modern psycho-

logical interpretation of dreams by his intuitive representation of the
subtle significances of their irrationality. In the opening lines the poet
reveals his method:

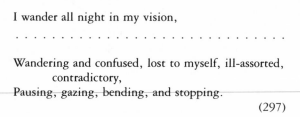

> I wander all night in my vision,
>
> . . . .
>
> Wandering and confused, lost to myself, ill-assorted,
>   contradictory,
> Pausing, gazing, bending, and stopping.
>
>   (297)

The substance of the poem consists of the chaotic cluster of images that
the poet collects in his vagabondage through the dreams of mankind.

Of the poem's eight sections, the first two and the last two form a
frame for the center four. The opening and the close of the poem consist
of fragmentary and broken images, of snatches and glimpses tumbled
forth in disordered heaps—connected only subterraneously, in the dim
recesses of the unconscious. The dramatic nature of the poem provides
this structure. The events cover one night, and the poet is portrayed
as falling into and emerging from his deep sleep. In the process of
going into and returning from the still trance of his deepest dreams,
he is caught up in a flow of fragmentary, disorganized dream-images.
But in the midst of his sleep, his dreams are lucid, sustained, vivid
reconstructions of an imagined reality.

In "going into" his dream trance, the poet becomes a series of things
and people in quick succession: "I am a dance—play up there! the fit
is whirling me fast!" (298). "I am the actor, the actress, the voter, the
politician, / The emigrant and the exile, the criminal that stood in the
box" (298). He becomes a girl receiving her lover in the darkness, a
sleepless widow, a shroud—"I wrap a body and lie in the coffin" (299).

Sections 3 and 4, in contrast with the first two, are lucid and co-
herent, a scene of shipwreck and disaster, with a vivid, detailed picture
of "a beautiful gigantic swimmer swimming naked through the eddies
of the sea" (299)—but finally borne away a corpse. These scenes of
death are followed in sections 5 and 6 by two unusual scenes of the
past. The first is of General Washington, in defeat at Brooklyn, and
then bidding fond farewell to his officers and men; the second is the
poet's mother as a young girl developing a strong "adhesive" attachment for a transient "red squaw" of "wonderful beauty and purity"

(300). These juxtaposed scenes of death and love, of brutal destruction and sympathetic attachment, serve as silent and affirmative commentary on each other.

Sections 7 and 8 revert to the fragmentary and disjointed quality of the opening sections: "A show of the summer softness—a contact of something unseen—an amour of the light and air" (301). Reality is distorted and twisted: "Elements merge in the night, ships make tacks in the dreams" (301). But emerging from the rapid flow of diverse images is the suggestion of night and sleep as the great levelers—for the sick and the homely as well as the "perfect-form'd" and the beautiful are "averaged": "The night and sleep have liken'd them and restored them" (301). The poem closes with the clear image of the night as the great womb of nature, of sleep as death: the entire poem becomes, on the symbolic level, an exploration of the world of spirituality.

Briefer Lyrics

An irony of Whitman's reputation is that he is most widely known by one of his least successful and most uncharacteristic poems: "O Captain! My Captain!" This poem, with its melodramatic statement of a public sentiment on a public occasion, suggests—when contrasted with the brilliant elegy "When Lilacs Last in the Dooryard Bloom'd"— that Whitman found the longer lyric forms more congenial for his expansive, free-flowing style. It is probably true that Whitman's greatest poetry is found in his longer poems, but there are many short poems throughout *Leaves* that have a brilliance and luster all their own.

Many of Whitman's frequently reprinted brief lyrics appear to be partially incomplete, not quite finished. The reason is that the short poems are usually firmly attached to their positions in the structure of *Leaves*. To remove them is to deprive them of part of their roots, for part of their meaning derives from their relationships with their environment. The opening poem of *Leaves*, "One's Self I Sing," is a poem of this kind. When Whitman says, "Of physiology from top to toe I sing," or "The Female equally with the Male I sing" (5), his reference is to the whole of his work; indeed, the very form of the phrase ("I sing") is meant to suggest the epic quality of *Leaves*.

This same principle applies to such a popular poem as "I Hear America Singing." Its position in "Inscriptions" indicates that it is announcing some of the themes of the *Leaves*. The poet concludes his catalog:

The delicious singing of the mother, or of the young
        wife at work, or of the girl sewing or washing,
Each singing what belongs to him or her and to none else,
The day what belongs to the day—at night the party of
        young fellows, robust, friendly,
Singing with open mouths their strong melodious songs.
                                                    (12–13)

These portraits of the "young wife" and the "young fellows," set one
against the other, are clearly related to the paired sections of *Leaves,*
"Children of Adam" and "Calamus." The "varied carols" the poet hears
are the carols he himself has written into his masterpiece. Similarly,
"When I Heard the Learn'd Astronomer" is modified in meaning by
its position near "I Sit and Look Out" in the "By the Roadside" section
of *Leaves.* After hearing the "astronomer where he lectured with much
applause in the lecture-room," the poet becomes "tired and sick" and
wanders off into the night and looks up "in perfect silence at the stars"
(196). This simple lyric might suggest that Whitman, like the other
romantics, attacked science as an enemy of the imagination. But the
attitude of silent observation, of detached contemplation, is a part of
the dominant mood and tone of "By the Roadside" (as in "I Sit and
Look Out"). Moreover, Whitman has already expressed complete and
unreserved acceptance of science in section 23 of "Song of Myself":

Hurrah for positive science! long live exact demonstration!
. . . .

Gentlemen, to you the first honors always!
Your facts are useful, and yet they are not my dwelling,
I but enter by them to an area of my dwelling.
                                                    (41)

"When I Heard the Learn'd Astronomer" is a dramatization fulfilling
this basic attitude.
    Some of Whitman's poems seem to be simply pictures, vignettes,
that have no more meaning than simply being themselves. In "My
Picture-Gallery" (in "Autumn Rivulets"), Whitman says:

In a little house keep I pictures suspended, it is not a
        fix'd house,
It is round, it is only a few inches from one side to the other;

> Yet behold, it has room for all the shows of the world, all
>   memories!
> Here the tableaus of life, and here the groupings of
>   death;
>
> (282)

Such "shows of the world," or "tableaus," seem to be scattered throughout *Leaves*. But a second and closer look frequently reveals some symbolic significance. For example, "The Dalliance of the Eagles" (in "By the Roadside") portrays the "rushing amourous contact" of two eagles:

> The clinching interlocking claws, a living, fierce, gyrating
>   wheel,
> Four beating wings, two beaks, a swirling mass tight
>   grappling,
> In tumbling turning clustering loops, straight downward
>   falling,
> Till o'er the river pois'd, the twain yet one, a moment's lull,
> A motionless still balance in the air, then parting, talons
>   loosing,
> Upward again on slow-firm pinions slanting, their separate
>   diverse flight,
> She hers, he his, pursuing.
>
> (198)

This simple "picture" contains in its symbolic drama the entire complex view of "Children of Adam"—the delirious abandon to the sexual merge, but with the persistence of personal identity and individuality. The poem gathers meaning, too, from section 32 of "Song of Myself"—"I think I could turn and live with animals, they are so placid and self-contain'd": "So they show their relations to me and I accept them, / They bring me tokens of myself, they evince them plainly in their possession" (47).

"Sparkles from the Wheel" (in "Autumn Rivulets") similarly seems to be simply a picture of a knife-grinder "at his wheel sharpening a great knife." The poem's substance consists mainly of the scene of the grinder at work, shooting out "copious golden jets," surrounded by a group of children—a tableau drawn from life's daily and passing scene. There are clues, however, to a more complex meaning. The poet seems strangely drawn to the scene: "Myself effusing and fluid, a phantom

curiously floating, now here absord'd and arrested." But the conclusion
seems merely to re-outline the scene:

> The group, (an unminded point set in a vast surrounding),
> The attentive, quiet children, the loud, proud, restive base
>   of the streets,
> The low hoarse purr of the whirling stone, the light-press'd
>   blade,
> Diffusing, dropping, sideways-darting, in tiny showers
>   of gold,
> Sparkles from the wheel.
>
> (275)

Does the poet see in the grinder an image of himself as artist—his
poetry sending off sparks to illuminate the world, to give glimpses
into the universe? When the poem is placed beside such poems as
"Eidólons" (7–10) in "Inscriptions," or such an ordinary poem as "Kosmos" (276–77) in "Autumn Rivulets," it becomes inescapably symbolic; the "copious golden jets" travel far beyond the immediate scene
into the "vast surrounding."

The problem of reading Whitman's poems biographically, the "I" as
the historical Walter Whitman, is exemplified in a number of poems
throughout *Leaves,* as for example "Vigil Strange I Kept on the Field
One Night" and "Prayer of Columbus." Although these poems embody
at some levels Whitman's feeling or emotions, they are dramatic solil-
oquies spoken by invented characters. The narrator of "Vigil Strange"
is a soldier caught up in the intensity and tragedy of battle who must,
at first, leave his fallen comrade on the field as he speeds onward in
the fight. But at the finish he finds him again, and the entire poem
consists of the ritualistic chant of soldier for his dead comrade, an
account of the "immortal and mystic hours" the soldier spent in spiritual communion with his fallen companion:

> Till at latest lingering of the night, indeed just as the
>   dawn appear'd,
> My comrade I wrapt in his blanket, envelop'd well his form,
> Folded the blanket well, tucking it carefully over head
>   and carefully under feet,

> And there and then and bathed by the rising sun, my son
> in his grave, in his rude-dug grave I deposited,
>
> (218)

The poem is remarkable for the effectiveness of its repetition in suggesting, without sentimentality, the depth of feeling of the soldier for his comrade.

Like "Vigil Strange," "Prayer of Columbus" is a dramatic soliloquy, the narrator a dramatic figure. Also like "Vigil Strange," "Prayer of Columbus" derives much of its meaning from its context in *Leaves*. It follows "Passage to India," a celebration of the final rounding of the globe that Columbus—here called the "chief histrion"—had attempted. In its proximity to "Passage to India," the poignancy of "Prayer of Columbus" is heightened. But it has an intensity of its own in its contrast of the outward condition of the explorer with his inner faith. He is a "batter'd, wreck'd old man," who is "sore, stiff with many toils, sicken'd and nigh to death." But his bitterness is dispelled in contemplation of God:

> I cannot rest O God, I cannot eat or drink or sleep,
> Till I put forth myself, my prayer, once more to Thee,
> Breathe, bathe myself once more in Thee, commune with
> Thee,
>
> (295)

The old man in his prayer gives expression to the mystic apprehension of the Deity that has marked his life:

> That Thou O God my life hast lighted,
> With ray of light, steady, ineffable, vouchsafed of Thee,
> Light rare untellable, lighting the very light,
> Beyond all signs, descriptions, languages;
>
> (296)

As in "Vigil Strange," the poet avoids sentimentality in dealing with a potentially sentimental subject by a complex union of devices, such as the chanted and ritualistic repetitions.

One of the most successful of Whitman's short poems is "A Noiseless Patient Spider," remarkable in both meaning and form. Its ten lines

are carefully divided into two stanzas: the first contains the picture;
the second makes explicit the symbolic meaning:

> A noiseless patient spider,
> I mark'd where on a little promontory it stood isolated,
> Mark'd how to explore the vacant vast surrounding,
> It launch'd forth filament, filament, filament, out of itself,
> Ever unreeling them, ever tirelessly speeding them.
>
> And you O my soul where you stand,
> Surrounded, detached, in measureless oceans of space,
> Ceaselessly musing, venturing, throwing, seeking the spheres
>   to connect them,
> Till the bridge you will need be form'd, till the ductile
>   anchor hold,
> Till the gossamer thread you fling catch somewhere,
>   O my soul.
>
>   (314)

The position of this poem in "Whispers of Heavenly Death" extends
its meaning far into the spiritual realm, suggesting that it deals not
only with human relationships, but also with the relationship to divinity in both life and death—the recurring theme of the cluster.

An early version of "A Noiseless Patient Spider" provides a remarkable (and perhaps astonishing) view of Whitman's creative genius at
work. This version was found in his notebooks:

> The Soul, reaching, throwing out for love,
> As the spider, from some little promontory, throwing out fila-
>   ment after filament, tirelessly out of itself, that one at least
>   may catch and form a link, a bridge, a connection
> O I saw one passing alone, saying hardly a word—yet full of
>   love I detected him, by certain signs
> O eyes wishfully turning! O silent eyes!
> For then I thought of you oer the world
> O latent oceans, fathomless oceans of love!
> O waiting oceans of love! yearning and fervid! and of you sweet
>   souls perhaps in the future, delicious and long:
> But Dead, unknown on the earth—ungiven, dark here, un-
>   spoken, never born:
> You fathomless latent souls of love—you pent and unknown
>   oceans of love![6]

Expressing essentially a "Calamus" or comradeship emotion, this early version of the poem is curiously weak, diffuse, and exclamatory. Whitman rescued the one brilliant image of the poem, the spider spinning his web; by reshaping it and extending it, he created one of his best poems. And then, by carefully placing it in the latter part of the *Leaves* among the "Whispers of Heavenly Death" poems, he further enriched and extended its meaning. In "A Noiseless Patient Spider," as in many of his short lyrics, Whitman demonstrated his mastery of both meaning and form in handling a big subject within a brief compass.

Chapter Six
Recurring Images

Because *Leaves of Grass* is something more than simply a collection of miscellaneous lyric poetry written over a lifetime, it offers many aesthetic gratifications to the reader who explores it as a unified whole. One of the devices that the structure makes possible, and which in turn contributes to the shaping of the structure, is the recurring image. Such images abound in *Leaves*; as they appear again and again they gather a body of meaning and a wealth of suggestion, until they develop into symbols of major significance for the poet—and the reader. Some of the most important of the recurring images are the grass, the sea, the bird, a whole cluster of celestial bodies, and others—such as the tree and the city. Any reader could compile his own list, and the diversity of the lists would simply reflect the complexity of the *Leaves* and its intricacy of design.

Grass

The dominant image in all of Whitman's work is the simple, separate leaf of grass. It is an image that gave him his title in his first edition in 1855, that served as a cluster-title in several subsequent editions, and that stuck to the end, without change, as the one single symbol that concentrated in itself the suggestion of the poet's many meanings. In the first edition *Leaves of Grass* appeared to be the title of every poem and appeared on every page as the running-title of the book.

Just how Whitman hit upon the term *leaves* in referring to blades of grass is not known. But that he was fully aware of the ambiguity and novelty of the word is clear. Throughout his book, he capitalizes on the merged meaning of the leaf as a common product of nature and as a page of his poetry. And he fuses the images of the blade of grass and the leaf of a tree, permitting himself to move from one to the other in successive poems without blurring his dominant image. In view of Whitman's theory of the suggestiveness of poetry, it would be misleading to define the symbolic meaning of the *leaves of grass* with precision. But many meanings closely related to Whitman's themes suggest themselves. Among them the most fundamental derives from the characteristic of grass to grow not only in single blades but also in clusters or clumps. The grass thus becomes a graphic representation of Whitman's central concept of democracy—individuality in balance with the mass, distinguished singleness in harmony with massive grouping.

The imagination of the reader will supply many related and supplementary meanings for the grass, especially on exploring "Song of Myself" as it incorporates the image in the basic foundations of its own (and the book's) structure. From the beginning of the poem, as the poet leans and loafs at his "ease observing a spear of summer grass," to the end, as he bequeaths himself to the "dirt to grow from the grass" he loves, the grass commands the poem's central position and directs its movement. It recurs not with mechanical regularity but in strategic sections where it springs to the fore with renewed life, and gathers the meaning of the poem into its slender, vital spears.

The spear of summer grass that the poet nonchalantly observes symbolizes in its simplicity the miracle of the universe. The mystery of life, of existence, of being, lies not far away in the exotic and mythical; it is in the near at hand, in the familiar and common. The spear of summer grass may therefore serve as the object of contemplation in launching the mystic journey. If the poet can apprehend the miraculous mystery of the silent, self-defined spear growing the globe around, he can then come to terms with the meaning of the universe. The one provides the key to the other: "I believe a leaf of grass is no less than the journey-work of the stars" (46).

In a sense, then, the leaf of grass has no limits in its symbolic meaning—it means *everything, all,* the *total.* When the poet specifically explores the variety of its meanings in section 6 of "Song of Myself," he confesses his own uncertainty:

> A child said *What is the grass?* fetching it to me with full
>   hands;
> How could I answer the child? I do not know what it is
>   any more than he.
>
> (28)

But the poet is willing to guess at some of the meanings. It may be the "flag" of his disposition, "out of hopeful green stuff woven." It may be the "handkerchief of the Lord," or it may itself be a child ("the produced babe of the vegetation"): "Or I guess it is a uniform hiero-glyphic, / And it means, Sprouting alike in broad zones and narrow zones" (28). Indeed, the grass may have as many meanings as there are spears, each one significant in its own right: "O I perceive after all so many uttering tongues, / And I perceive they do not come from the roofs of mouths for nothing" (29).

Outside "Song of Myself," the grass appears and reappears, some-times merely mentioned, sometimes presented in full portrait; but it always carries along the complex of meaning that has accrued. It is surely the floor of the renewed "garden" of the "Children of Adam" poems; it certainly appears along the "Open Road" which the poet takes to "afoot and light-hearted." It survives even its embracement in French in "Our Old Feuillage." It provides the bed for the "Broad-Axe" to lie upon ("Resting the grass amid and upon"), and it must provide the seat for the poet as he sits observing "By the Roadside."

In these and in other places throughout the *Leaves* the grass is glimpsed, subtly injecting its slender shape and green color. But prob-ably the most dramatic variation in the use of the image is in the "Calamus" section. When queried about calamus by someone who did not know the plant, Whitman replied: "Calamus is the very large and aromatic grass, or rush, growing about water ponds in the valleys—spears about three feet high; often called Sweet Flag; grows all over the Northern and Middle States. The recherché or ethereal sense of the term, as used in my book, arises probably from the actual Calamus presenting the biggest and hardiest kind of spears of grass, and their fresh, aquatic, pungent *bouquet*."[1] This was the symbol that the poet wished to identify with the theme of adhesiveness, or comradeship. In contrast with the common grass "that grows wherever the land is and the water is" (37), the calamus plant grows "In paths untrodden, / In the growth by margins of pond-waters, / Escaped from the life that exhibits itself" (84).

The true calamus-relationship is rare, exceptional, uncommon. As the poet elaborates the image in such poems as "Scented Herbage of My Breast" and "These I Singing in Spring," he exploits all the pos-sibilities for symbolism that the strongly individualistic plant offers—"Indeed O death, I think now these leaves mean precisely the same as you mean" (85), "And this, O this shall henceforth be the token of comrades, this calamus-root shall" (88). Anyone familiar with the long, tapering leaves and the cylindrical flower of the calamus plant will recognize the phallic symbolism immediately. Whitman seemed to acknowledge the ambiguity of the image in "Scented Herbage of My Breast" when he exclaimed: "Emblematic and capricious blades I leave you, now you serve me not, / I will say what I have to say by itself" (85). The outcry is, of course, merely a part of the poem's drama, and its ultimate consequence is to emphasize the spirituality (as suggested by the "pungent *bouquet*" of the calamus) of the "manly attachment" celebrated by the poet as the basis of genuine democracy.

The Sea

Probably no image, not even that in the title, appears more frequently in *Leaves of Grass* than the sea and the related water images such as rivers, lakes, and ponds. The image is established almost from the beginning as a major symbol; certainly by the time one has read through the introductory pages, he has become aware of the important role that the sea is to assume in the poetry that follows.

The third poem in "Inscriptions," "In Cabin'd Ships at Sea," introduces the image: "The boundless blue on every side expanding, / With whistling winds and music of the waves, the large imperious waves" (6). And the mariners, or voyagers, in their contemplation of the poet's "reminiscence of the land," assert that they *"feel"* the *"ebb and flow of endless motion," "the vague and vast suggestions of the briny world, the liquid-flowing syllables"* (6). In this poem the land-ocean dichotomy, which functions symbolically (along with that point of union, the seashore) throughout *Leaves of Grass,* is vividly introduced. Although *Leaves of Grass* is *"ocean's poem,"* it is also land's poem—it is the poem of both the body and the soul.

After its sporadic appearance in the song section of *Leaves,* the sea image become dominant in the "Sea-Drift" cluster. As the title of this section indicates, emphasis is placed on one attribute of the sea—the refuse thrown up by the waves to the shallow waters of the seashore. And of course the poet intends, as applicable to himself and to mankind, all of the connotations of the word "drift." The word suggests the quality of questioning restlessness which seems to define the poet's emotional state in the poems throughout the section. But although "Out of the Cradle Endlessly Rocking" (the first poem) is a "sea-shore" poem, the only "drift" cast up by the ocean in it is the word *death:*

> But edging near as privately for me rustling at my feet,
> Creeping thence steadily up to my ears and laving me
>   softly all over,
> Death, death, death, death, death.
>
>   (184)

There seems to be here an enactment of the death scene, with the sea
assuming the role of death. But the sea is identified as a "cradle endlessly rocking" in the opening line of the poem, and the metaphor is
repeated at the end—"old crone rocking the cradle, swathed in sweet
garments, bending aside" (184). This vivid figure is inevitably associated with the word whispered out of the sea: *death*. The poet, through
the association of images, links birth with death, death with birth.
Because of his realization that the two are closely linked, that death is
not an end but a beginning, the poet accepts the word *death* as the
"word of the sweetest song."

Although the sea is described as "the fierce old mother" who "endlessly cries for her castaways" in "As I Ebb'd with the Ocean of Life,"
the central symbol is "The rim, the sediment that stands for all the
water and all the land of the globe" (185). As in "In Cabin'd Ships at
Sea," the poet utilizes both land and sea as major symbols. The seashore
becomes the meeting ground for body and spirit, life and death; but
it is a meeting ground ambiguous in meaning because of the "tufts of
straw, sands, fragments" which are "Buoy'd hither from many moods,
one contradicting another." But when the poet asserts, "I too have
bubbled up, floated the measureless float, and been wash'd on your
shores" (186), he seems to acknowledge an awareness of his origin in
the world of spirit and his ultimate, perhaps imminent, return.

After its full exploitation in "Sea-Drift," the sea or water image
appears frequently in *Leaves of Grass*. In "When Lilacs Last in the Dooryard Bloom'd," it is "Down to the shores of the water, the path by the
swamp in the dimness" (237) that the poet is finally lured by the hermit-thrush and "death's outlet song of life." And as the poet listens,
the bird's song *"float[s]" "over the rising and sinking waves"* (238). In "By
Blue Ontario's Shore," what was once the 1855 Preface has been translated into poetry and given a seminarrative framework and a setting
beside a large body of water. Ontario's shore gains significance from
the seashore symbolism of the "Sea-Drift" section. There is the clear
suggestion that the poet's spiritual insight is related to his position by
the waters of Ontario:

> Thus by blue Ontario's shore,
> While the winds fann'd me and the waves came trooping
>   toward me,
> I thrill'd with the power's pulsations, and the charm of
>   my theme was upon me,
> Till the tissues that held me parted their ties upon me.
>
> (251)

The poet here dramatizes a spiritual trance; and Ontario's shore, its winds and waves, play a vital role in bestowing the vision.

The "Autumn Rivulets" section of *Leaves* incorporates the symbolic water image in its title. And the opening poem, "As Consequent, Etc.," asserts that "life's ever-modern rapids" are "soon to blend, / With the old streams of death": "In you whoe'er you are my book perusing, / In I myself, in all the world, these currents flowing, / All, all toward the mystic ocean tending" (253). The "mystic ocean" is the realm of the spirit, as the reader of *Leaves* by now already knows. The poet also makes further use in this poem of the seashore symbol exploited in "Sea-Drift": "Currents for starting a continent new, / Overtures sent to the solid out of the liquid, / Fusion of ocean and land, tender and pensive waves" (253). Those "overtures" sent out of the liquid could be none other than a spiritual wooing which, in turn, seems to culminate in the "fusion" of water and earth represented by the seashore. Such a fusion is a marriage of body and soul, of the material and the spiritual, of life and death.

"Passage to India" makes full use of the ocean as symbol in the central dramatic situation of the poem, in which the poet pleads with his soul to venture forth on the voyage. Near the end the poet exclaims:

> Sail forth—steer for the deep waters only,
> Reckless O soul, exploring, I with thee, and thou with me,
> For we are bound where mariner has not yet dared
>   to go,
>
> (294)

The place for which the poet and his soul are bound is, surely, the country of death—the realm of the spirit. Or, as the poet says a few lines later, "O daring joy, but safe! are they not all the seas of God?" (294).

The seas throughout *Leaves of Grass* are "the seas of God." "What

Ship Puzzled at Sea," in the "Whispers of Heavenly Death" section, utilizes the sea as symbol to dramatize the situation of an individual spiritually lost and in need of direction. The poet says, "Here, sailor! here, ship! take aboard the most perfect pilot" (313), referring to himself and his book. In the "Songs of Parting" section, use is made of the sea image in two poems of farewell, "Joy, Shipmate, Joy!" and "Now Finalè to the Shore." And throughout the annexes, the sea maintains its position as a dominant image in Whitman's poetry. Almost the entire symbolic significance of such a slight poem as "From Montauk Point" (in "Sands at Seventy") is dependent on the meanings the sea accumulates throughout *Leaves*. The poet looks out and contemplates

> The tossing waves, the foam, the ships in the distance,
> The wild unrest, the snowy, curling caps—that inbound
>   urge and urge of waves,
> Seeking the shores forever.
>
>   (351)

Although in *Leaves* the sea and other water images invariably are associated with the soul and the world of spirituality, their contexts frequently suggest more complex meanings. Sigmund Freud, in his discussion of dream imagery, asserted that birth almost always is associated with water—either the entering of it or the emerging from it. He conjectured that the reason for this association is twofold: first, there is a racial memory, unconscious, of the evolutionary emergence of life from the sea; and second, there is a personal memory, quite likely unconscious, of an individual's emergence from the embryo stage in the amniotic liquid of the womb.[2] Throughout *Leaves*, water is associated with death; but in Whitman's view, death is birth, a rebirth, an entry into the spiritual world comparable to the previous entry into the physical world. In "Out of the Cradle Endlessly Rocking," the identification of the sea with the crone rocking the cradle appears to associate the ocean with the amniotic fluid of the womb and is suggestive of the ocean as the evolutionary source of all life. With birth and life came also, as the old crone of the sea whispers ("hissing melodious" like the snake of the Garden of Eden), "death, death, death, death, death" (184). There is suggested, then, the cyclic paradox: life brings death; death brings life.[3]

The Bird

The bird image is first introduced in "Starting from Paumanok." The mockingbird, the thrush, and hawk—the birds Whitman writes about most frequently—all appear:

> Having studied the mocking-bird's tones and the flight
>   of the mountain-hawk,
> And heard at dawn the unrivall'd one, the hermit-thrush
>   from the swamp-cedars,
> Solitary, singing in the West, I strike up for a New
>   World.
>
>   (15)

In the introduction the poet places emphasis on particular distinguishing details that are to have greatest significance in the dramatic roles to be played later by the birds—the song of the mockingbird, the flight of the mountain-hawk, the habitat (swamp-cedars) of the hermit-thrush. And the poet is careful to capitalize on the connotations implicit in the adjectival elements in the names of these birds: *mocking, mountain, hermit.*

Between its introduction in "Starting from Paumanok" and its major symbolic use in "Birds of Passage" and "Out of the Cradle Endlessly Rocking," the bird image appears only sporadically. At the end of "Song of Myself," in the famous "barbaric yawp" passage, the poet identifies himself and his primitive nature with the hawk. Vivid use is made of the bird image in a "Children of Adam" poem, "We Two, How Long We Were Fool'd"; in these two poems, hawks symbolize the realization of the transcendent fulfillment of primitive, natural, and uninhibited sexuality. In "Crossing Brooklyn Ferry," sea gulls are among the "dumb, beautiful ministers" that furnish their "parts toward eternity" (120).

But it is not until the "Birds of Passage" section that the bird image comes clearly to the fore. In the opening poem of the section, "Song of the Universal," the "uncaught bird," ever "hovering, hovering, / High in the purer, happier air" (166) is one of several images used to symbolize the presence of future perfection within the imperfect now. By "spiral routes" this seed of perfection will eventually reach fulfillment, as all things tend toward the ideal in "mystic evolution" (166).

All events in time are, like the flights of birds, simply happenings in the unfolding of mystic evolution; these events have significance only in "passage"—that is, only in their contribution to time's unraveling. Also, events unfold rhythmically (on "spiral routes"), just as the flights of birds are recurrent, patterned after the rhythmical rotation of the seasons.

In "Out of the Cradle Endlessly Rocking," the bird is for the first time given a major dramatic role. The mockingbirds in "Out of the Cradle Endlessly Rocking" are "two feather'd guests from Alabama" (180) whose domestic bliss is destroyed by the disappearance of the she-bird. As the small boy listens, the he-bird pours forth his great, sad carol of "*lonesome love*" (182). Were the song no more than a lament of the bereaved lover, the poem would still be a masterpiece. But the mockingbird's outcry of bereavement has a special significance: "The aria's meaning" (183) deposited in the soul of the boy is never explicitly stated but it is hinted at when the poet exclaims: "The messenger there arous'd, the fire, the sweet hell within, / The unknown want, the destiny of me" (184). The mockingbird symbolizes the creative transfiguration brought by consuming but unfulfilled love. And when the sea sends forth its word of death as the "clew" the boy requests, the "outsetting bard" has found the theme for all his songs.

In "When Lilacs Last in the Dooryard Bloom'd," the poet makes full use of the attributes of the bird chosen to play a major role in the poem: "Solitary the thrush, / The hermit withdrawn to himself, avoiding the settlements, / Sings by himself a song" (233). The bird sings, in the "secluded recesses" of the swamp, his "song of the bleeding throat." The poet quickly realizes that the bird's song will effect a reconciliation to the lamented death, but he tells the "bashful and tender" singer, "But a moment I linger, for the lustrous star has detain'd me" (235). His grief over the death of Lincoln spent, the poet flees to the swamp to listen to and translate the thrush's song. The song turns out to be a paean in praise of "*the sure-enwinding arms of cool-enfolding death*" (237), a carol of joy at the bliss of death. The insight granted the poet in "Out of the Cradle Endlessly Rocking," where he fuses the bird's song and the sea's word, is in "Lilacs" granted by the bird's song alone. After the song of the hermit-thrush the poet is granted a mystic vision that assures him of the joy of death. In initiating this reconciliation, the thrush represents the voice of spirituality. Like the "uncaught bird" of "Song of the Universal," the hermit-thrush in "Lilacs" is the spiritual that exists in the present imperfection (or grief), the impulse toward the ideal that is the hope in the tragedy of death.

Near the end of *Leaves of Grass,* in "Thou Mother with Thy Equal Brood," the poet envisions the nation itself as a bird in flight:

> As a strong bird on pinions free,
> Joyous, the amplest spaces heavenward cleaving,
> Such be the thought I'd think of thee America,
> Such be the recitative I'd bring for thee.
>
> (317)

The figure seems apt for the view that America's promise must find its fulfillment in the future: "Shalt soar toward the fulfillment of the future, the spirit of the body and the mind, / The soul, its destinies" (320). The figure of the bird is here again used to suggest the hidden if not secret resource of mystic evolution. America is like the hovering "uncaught bird" of "Song of the Universal."

In view of the various symbolic functions of the bird image in *Leaves,* the systematic introduction of the three birds—mockingbird, mountain-hawk, hermit-thrush—in "Starting from Paumanok" may have special significance. Later in the poem the poet cries out the greatness of another trinity:

> My comrade!
> For you to share with me two greatnesses, and a third one
>   rising inclusive and more resplendent,
> The greatness of Love and Democracy, and the greatness
>   of Religion.
>
> (19)

Whitman's three birds seem clearly to relate to his three themes:

> Mockingbird—Love
> Mountain-hawk—Democracy
> Hermit-thrush—Religion[4]

Poems in *Leaves of Grass* in which these birds are most fully portrayed bear out their association with particular themes: the mockingbird with love, both fulfilled and "lonesome," in "Out of the Cradle End-

lessly Rocking"; the mountain-hawk (or eagle or sea gull with which
the hawk, in its attribute of soaring flight, is associated) with democracy in "Thou Mother with Thy Equal Brood" (once called "As a Strong
Bird on Pinions Free"); and the hermit-thrush with religion (or spirituality) in "When Lilacs Last in the Dooryard Bloom'd." Most frequently throughout *Leaves of Grass* the bird image is, like the hermit-
thrush in "Lilacs," a "santa spirita" figure (the "light, lighter than
light" in "Chanting the Square Deific"[309–11]), reminding the poet
by its presence and its notes, no matter how small or low, of the eternal
in the temporal, of the spiritual beyond the material.

Celestial Bodies

The earth, sun; moon, and star appear separately or, frequently, in
groups in the celestial scenes of *Leaves*. For example, in "Eidólons":

> All space, all time,
> (The stars, the terrible perturbations of the suns,
> Swelling, collapsing, ending, serving their longer,
>   shorter use,)
> Fill'd with eidólons only.
>
>   (9)

A sky scene is evoked by the very words *space* and *time,* and the gradual
evolution of the celestial destiny is cited as "proof" of the existence of
the spiritual (and guiding) world of eidólons. Perhaps the most im-
pressive scene of this kind in Whitman is in "Song of Myself":

> I open my scuttle at night and see the far-sprinkled systems,
> And all I see multiplied as high as I can cipher edge but
>   the rim of the farther systems.
>
> Wider and wider they spread, expanding, always expanding,
> Outward and outward and forever outward.
>
> My sun has his sun and round him obediently wheels,
> He joins with his partners a group of superior circuit,
> And greater sets follow, making specks of the greatest
>   inside them.
>
>   (63)

The immense, far-flung, and endless "superior circuits" serve to imply to man, in his quest for order in a chaotic world, that his disorder is part of a greater harmony. The balance and rhythm of an infinite universe are the basis for a faith in a cosmic plan in which man serves his purpose. Paradoxically, that universe, which shrinks not just man but his solar system into microscopic specks by its order and complexly intricate interrelationships, makes man and his destiny supremely important in an unfolding cosmic scheme.

The earth frequently appears in *Leaves* as a great round globe sailing through the heavens. This perspective serves to project both poet and reader into the universe as cosmic observers witnessing the dramatic progression of the earth. For example: "Earth, my likeness, / Though you look so impassive, ample and spheric there, / I now suspect that is not all" (96). The *there* (end of the second line) suggests a gesture of pointing by the poet to a globe from which he has somehow cast himself adrift. Curiously enough, it is almost always this independent view of the earth that appears in *Leaves*. Some of Whitman's most interesting effects are achieved by dramatic changes in perspective involving this "spheric" earth. In "Salut au Monde!" for instance, the poet passes from a point of observation on the earth to one out in space and then, finally, to a position back on the earth. As the poet observes from afar the ball of earth, he seems to assume the magnitude of a deity: "I see a great round wonder rolling through space . . . / I see the shaded part on one side where the sleepers are sleeping, and the sunlit part on the other side" (101). Such a view of the earth, reduced in size to the scale of a child's toy, results in a corresponding enlargement of the observer. As the earth comes within the grasp of the on-looker, so the individual assumes a position of greater magnitude in the universe. Such a result seems clearly the intent of the poet; in "A Song of the Rolling Earth" he says: "Whoever you are! motion and reflection are especially for you, / The divine ship sails the divine sea for you" (163).

Because of its appearance in "When Lilacs Last in the Dooryard Bloom'd," the star is perhaps the best known of the celestial images in Whitman. The drama of the dark cloud obscuring the bright star is, however, a recurring symbolic event in *Leaves*. The drama first appears in "On the Beach at Night":

> Up through the darkness,
> While ravening clouds, the burial clouds, in black
>   masses spreading,

Lower sullen and fast athwart and down the sky,
Amid a transparent clear belt of ether yet left in the east,
Ascends large and calm the lord-star Jupiter,

(188)

The father assures the frightened child that the "ravening clouds" obscure the stars "only in apparition." In "When Lilacs Last in the Dooryard Bloom'd," the same symbolic drama recurs. In the opening of the poem the poet grieves:

O powerful western fallen star!
O shades of night—O moody, tearful night!
O great star disappear'd—O the black murk that hides
    the star!

(233)

Later in the poem, this "harsh surrounding cloud" is identified directly with the long funeral procession bearing the president's body from east to west: "Falling upon them all and among them all, enveloping me with the rest, / Appear'd the cloud, appear'd the long black trail" (236). This recurring image receives climactic treatment in one of the key poems in the latter part of *Leaves of Grass*—"Whispers of Heavenly Death":

I see, just see skyward, great cloud-masses,
Mournfully slowly they roll, silently swelling and mixing,
With at times a half-dimm'd sadden'd far-off star,
Appearing and disappearing.

(309)

It is clear that this simple but vivid celestial image signified for the poet the rebirth that is inherent in death. By their very nature—the star in its fixedness and the cloud in its transience—these heavenly objects symbolize the triumph of the eternal, the illusoriness of death.

The sun figures in a number of poems in *Leaves*. In "Crossing Brooklyn Ferry," the "sun there half an hour high" (116) becomes an important part of the dynamic setting. In section 3, at the opening of the scene, the sun's reflection forms the "fine centrifugal spokes" (117) of a halo for the poet as he gazes down into the water; but gradually the sun disappears, day fades, and by the end of the scene it is night. In "Out of the Cradle Endlessly Rocking," the sun is the most important figure in the first, happy song of the bird: *"Pour down your warmth, great sun! / While we bask, we two together"* (180). The sun in both of these poems is associated with fruitful, fulfilled life.

As some such symbol the sun receives its fullest treatment in the "Drum-Taps" poem, "Give Me the Splendid Silent Sun":

> Give me the splendid silent sun with all his beams full-dazzling,
> Give me juicy autumnal fruit ripe and red from the orchard,
> Give me a field where the unmow'd grass grows,
> Give me an arbor, give me the trellis'd grape,
>
> (223)

The sun in this poem is associated with the rich fertility of the orchard, grass, fruit—with unhampered nature in all its varied abundance. But the sun is more than the symbol of fertility; it is also the symbol of the "primal sanities" of solitude and nature. The sun thus symbolizes a way of life contrasted in the poem with the crowded and noisy "life of the theatre, bar-room, huge hotel" (224). In section 2 of the poem, beginning with the startling "Keep your splendid silent sun," the poet asserts his preference for the life of the cities, for the life of the war itself with its human tumult and impact.

The section of *Leaves of Grass* called "From Noon to Starry Night" utilizes in its title the sun as a symbol of fertility. In the opening poem of the section, "Thou Orb Aloft Full-Dazzling," the poet identifies the fruitfulness of the "hot October noon" with his own productivity as an artist; and he suggests that the poetic process, like the sun, has its "perturbations, sudden breaks and shafts of flame gigantic" (322). But the "fructifying heat and light" of the poet must eventually dissipate, as "noon" gives way to "starry night" (322). One of the poems in "Songs of Parting"—"Song at Sunset"—uses the sun as symbol in much the same way as "From Noon to Starry Night." When the poet says, "Splendor of ended day floating and filling me" (343), he is suggesting again the sun as symbol of creativity. As the sun sets in splendor, so the poet feels the magnificence of his last creative impulses. He pledges to sing until the "last ray gleams."

There is one "picture" that recurs in *Leaves of Grass* with so little variation in detail that one wonders whether it might not originate in an experience indelibly impressed on the poet's mind. The scene is most elaborately delineated in "Dirge for Two Veterans," a "Drum-Taps" poem, which describes the funeral for two soldiers, father and

son. The poet meticulously avoids sentimentality by focusing not on
the pathos but on the details of setting. Of these, the moon is the most
prominent:

> Lo, the moon ascending,
> Up from the east the silvery round moon,
> Beautiful over the house-tops, ghastly, phantom moon,
> Immense and silent moon.
>
> (224)

The moon serves in some mystic way to reconcile the poet to the tragic
deaths he witnesses. At one point he says that it is "Some mother's
large transparent face, / In heaven brighter growing" (225). And he
exclaims, "O moon immense with your silvery face you soothe me!"
(225). The moon also seems to transfigure death and diminish its hor-
ror in another "Drum-Taps" poem, "Look Down Fair Moon":

> Look down fair moon and bathe this scene,
> Pour softly down night's nimbus floods on faces ghastly,
>   swollen, purple,
> On the dead on their backs with arms toss'd wide,
> Pour down your unstinted nimbus sacred moon.
>
> (228)

Perhaps the secret of this obsessive scene is revealed in "Old War-
Dreams," in the "From Noon to Starry Night" section. The poet confesses, as the title suggests, that although the "carnage" through which
he moved has long since passed away, now he dreams "of their forms
at night." He dreams

> Of scenes of Nature, fields and mountains,
> Of skies so beauteous after a storm, and at night the
>   moon so unearthly bright,
> Shining sweetly, shining down, where we dig the trenches
>   and gather the heaps,
>   I dream, I dream, I dream.
>
> (336)

This scene of "the dead on their backs with arms extended wide" (336)
seems almost a precise duplication of that in "Look Down Fair Moon";
and the moon of "unearthly brightness" shedding its soothing nimbus

seems to be an image common to all of these battlefield scenes. The refrain, "I dream, I dream, I dream," suggests that the experience is so deeply imbedded in the poet's consciousness that not even the embodiment of the scene in art can purge it. If Whitman did derive the scene from some experience in the Civil War, it was a scene he was in part prepared for; for even before the war, in one of his most celebrated poems, "Out of the Cradle Endlessly Rocking," he had associated the moon ("The yellow half-moon enlarged, sagging down, drooping, the face of the sea almost touching" [183]) with death. The mockingbird in the poem, in his first song, invests the sun with his own feelings of a fulfilled, happy life; and, in his second "aria," he invests the moon with his keen sense of tragic loss in death. Underlying these identifications is, of course, the common association of the day with life, the night with death.

The Tree and the City

Many additional images recur throughout the *Leaves* and gather a special significance as they appear and reappear. Each reader will carry from the book memory of particular images that made vivid impressions. Not many readers, however, will miss Whitman's individual use of the tree and the city. These by no means exhaust the memorable images of *Leaves,* but they are representative. A glance at Whitman's handling of them should reveal, therefore, much of his method in using imagery throughout the whole of *Leaves.*

The tree was at one time destined to have a larger role in *Leaves.* Whitman at first wrote many of the "Calamus" poems under the title "Live Oak, with Moss," and this tree apparently once held the symbolic position now held by the calamus plant in the "Calamus" poems.[5] There are elements of this original plan that have survived. In "Starting from Paumanok," in the section that commands the reader to *see* in the poet's poems the whole varied life of the New World, Whitman says: "See, pastures and forests, in my poems—see, animals wild and tame—see, beyond the Kaw, countless herds of buffalo feeding on short curly grass" (23). In this slight reference to forests, Whitman merges them with other elements of the West to balance the "cities, solid, vast, inland, with paved streets" of the immediately succeeding line. In "Song of Myself," however, it is clear that the trees have acquired a symbolic function. "Earth of the slumbering and liquid trees" (39) is a line in the midst of a passionate passage in which the feminine earth

is described as awaiting her lover, the poet. In another passage nature
is described in sexual terms: "Broad muscular fields, branches of live
oak, loving lounger in my winding paths, it shall be you!" (42). There
seems no doubt that the tree has become identified in these passages
with the procreative processes of life.

This identification is suggested in "I Saw in Louisiana a Live-Oak
Growing," one of the survivors of the original series on the live-oak in
the "Calamus" section. The look of the live-oak, "rude, unbending,
lusty," makes the poet think of himself; and he breaks off "a twig with
a certain number of leaves upon it," twines "around it a little moss,"
and brings it home to place in his room. Both this token and the live-
oak itself ("the live-oak glistens there in Louisiana solitary in a wide
flat space") seem clearly phallic symbols. The poet himself says, "Yet
it remains to me a curious token, it makes me think of manly love"
(93). Like the calamus root, the tree in this case seems to be a physical
symbol of a spiritual love, that love which transcends the earthly love
of man and woman.

In "Our Old Feuillage" trees are a vivid part of the multitude of
images that constitute the "divine leaves" of the poet:

> In lower latitudes in warmer air in the Carolinas the
>   large black buzzard floating slowly high beyond
>   the tree tops,
> Below, the red cedar festoon'd with tylandria, the pines
>   and cypresses growing out of the white sand that
>   spreads far and flat,
>
> (126)

And trees are inevitably included in the cast of characters in "Song of
the Broad-Axe": "Welcome are lands of pine and oak, / Welcome are
lands of the lemon and fig . . ." (135). But in this poem, it is as
victims that the trees fulfill their function in the progression of events:
"The solid forest gives fluid utterances, / They tumble forth, they rise
and form . . ." (140). Their destiny, like man's, is a death and rebirth;
the "real" fulfillment arrives only with the rebirth.

It is, of course, as symbol of the wilderness and of the West that the
trees appear in "Song of the Broad-Axe," and it is as such a symbol
that the tree becomes the protagonist in "Song of the Redwood Tree,"
the only long poem devoted exclusively to this image. Whitman uses
the device of the personified redwood tree, in the throes of death, to

prophesy the accomplishment in the West of "the promise of thousands of years, till now deferr'd, / Promis'd to be fulfill'd, our common kind, the race" (154). In the description of the life experienced by the dying tree, the poem becomes clearly symbolic. The tree sings:

> *Perennial hardy life of me with joys 'mid rain and many*
>   *a summer sun,*
> *And the white snows and night and the wild winds;*
> *O the great patient rugged joys, my soul's strong joys*
>   *unreck'd by man,*
>
>   (151)

The "white snows" and "wild winds" are suggestive of turbulent human emotions; and, in the context of the symbolic significance of the tree in the previous pages of *Leaves,* the description of the habitat becomes more meaningful:

> *But come from Nature's long and harmless throes, peacefully*
>   *builded thence,*
> *These virgin lands, lands of the Western shore,*
> *To the new culminating man, to you, the empire new,*
>
>   (152)

This dedication of the "virgin lands" to the "new culminating man" suggests a feminine-masculine relationship perhaps symbolized by the tree itself on the lands. Such a suggestion seems reinforced as the tree continues to sing:

> *You occult deep volitions,*
> *You average spiritual manhood, purpose of all, pois'd*
>   *on yourself, giving not taking law,*
> *You womanhood divine, mistress and source of all, whence*
>   *life and love and ought that comes from life*
>   *and love,*
>
>   (152)

The "occult deep volitons," perhaps the life-force manifested in the sex instinct, seem to be symbolized by the masculine tree, poised and independent, and by the feminine earth, mistress and source of all. The earlier identification of the live-oak as a phallic symbol appears to be

exploited in the portrayal of other trees as complex symbols of the
frontier West.

Unlike many romantic poets, Whitman does not place a premium
on nature at the expense of the human. Whenever Whitman sketches
the city image in a few brief strokes, the reader feels his sense of excitement and awe and pleasure. Perhaps the equality with which Whitman viewed both country and city may be best seen in the opening
passage of "Starting from Paumanok," in which the poet presents himself as a composite American born of both city and the frontier. Not
only is he the "lover of populous pavements" and the "Dweller in
Mannahatta," but he is also a "miner in California" and roams "Da-
kota's woods"—". . . withdrawn to muse and meditate in some deep
recess, / Far from the clank of crowds intervals passing rapt and happy"
(15). When Whitman ends this passage with "Solitary, singing in the
West, I strike up for a New World" (15), the *West* is not the prairies
or the Pacific coast, but all these states that make up, in their populous
cities as well as their vast empty prairies, the New World.

Whitman had a genius for evoking in the fewest possible words the
busy, noisy, peopled city: "populous pavements," "the clank of
crowds." In the first the single detail chosen—pavements—is precisely
right for the dominant visual impression of a large city. In the second
the "clank" captures the dominant audioimpression. In a section of
"Song of Myself" (beginning the "blab of the pave"), Whitman suc-
ceeds admirably in a minimum of lines in evoking the entire complex
and exciting life of a city by the rapid listing, one after the other, of
evocative details—the "heavy omnibus," the "snow-sleighs," the
"rous'd mobs," the "curtain'd litter," the "meeting of enemies" with
the "excited crowd" penetrated by the policeman:

> The impassive stones that receive and return so many echoes,
> What groans of over-fed or half-starv'd who fall sunstruck
>   or in fits,
> What exclamations of women taken suddenly who hurry
>   home and give birth to babes,
> What living and buried speech is always vibrating here,
>   what howls restrain'd by decorum,
> Arrests of criminals, slights, adulterous offers made,
>   acceptances, rejections with convex lips,
>
>   (30)

These images, all the "echoes" of the "impassive stones," are designed
for the ear; they are also an extension of the opening image, "the blab
of the pave." Through these images of sound, Whitman recreates the
infinite and varied life of the city, not through an indiscriminate piling
of detail on detail but rather through careful selection of details which
combine to convey the essence of the immense and hurried city. And
Whitman does not portray the city in order to reject it. He says, "I
mind them or the show or resonance of them—I come and I depart"
(30).

Whitman was always able to evoke the turbulent and chaotic city in
a few vivid words. In "In Paths Untrodden" he says, "Here by myself
away from the clank of the world" (84). In "Song of the Open Road"
he says, "You flagg'd walks of the cities! you strong curbs at the edges!"
(109). In "Song of the Broad-Axe," he explains that the great city is
"not the place of stretch'd wharves, docks, manufactures, deposits of
produce merely," but rather the city which "stands with the brawniest
breed of orators and bards" (138). "A Broadway Pageant" takes place
when "million-footed Manhattan unpent descends to her pavements"
(177). In "First O Songs for a Prelude," the opening song of "Drum-
Taps," Manhattan is personified in a dramatic scene:

> Sleepless amid her ships, her houses, her incalculable wealth,
> With her million children around her, suddenly,
> At dead of night, at news from the south,
> Incens'd struck with clinch'd hand the pavement.
>
> (201)

In "Give Me the Splendid Silent Sun," half the poem is devoted to the
portrayal of the poet's beloved Manhattan, "People, endless, stream-
ing, with strong voices, passions, pageants" (224). In this poem Whitman's theme is his preference for the populous city over the solitude of
nature.

Something of Whitman's vast affection for his native town, the city
which, no doubt, served as the prototype for all the cities in *Leaves,* is
embodied in "Mannahatta" (in "From Noon to Starry Night"), a poem
unashamedly dedicated to the celebration of the metropolis:

> Trottoirs throng'd, vehicles, Broadway,
>   the women, the shops and shows,

A million people—manners free and superb
—open voices—hospitality—the
most courageous and friendly young men,
(330)

If Whitman's attitude toward the city as seen in "Give Me the Splendid
Silent Sun" was shaped by his faith in the cause of the Civil War and
his belief in the necessity of mass action, so his attitude in "Mannahatta"—and no doubt in other poems celebrating the city—is formed
in part out of his strong emotional devotion to the "Calamus" idea.
Companionship, friendship, comradeship, or the potential of such relationships existent in masses of people—all were for Whitman strong
attractions of the city of a million people. It is significant that the ideal
delineated in "Calamus," in the poem called "I Dream'd in a Dream,"
is, paradoxically, not an ideal of secluded nature as the "Calamus" symbol would suggest, but rather the ideal of a city—"the new city of
Friends" (96). But in addition the city attracted because it offered the
full rich complexity, multiplicity, comedy, and tragedy of life.

Even in "Sands at Seventy" Whitman could envision the romance of
the city with excitement: "(Could but thy flagstones, curbs, facades,
tell their inimitable tales; / Thy windows rich, and huge hotels—thy
sidewalks wide;)" (360). Men and women were, after all, the supreme
fact for Whitman. The universe of *Leaves* is human-centered, even
though there is full acceptance of science which paradoxically proves
otherwise. It is only natural that one of Whitman's most frequently
recurring images should be the populous city—the dwelling place of
individuals en masse. And the detail that appears almost invariably—
the sidewalk or pavement—suggests not individuals comfortably sit-
uated in their homes but people in movement, energetic and creative,
traveling the open, and endless, road.

Chapter Seven
Language and Wit

When Whitman remarked to Horace Traubel, "I sometimes think the *Leaves* is only a language experiment,"[1] he was expressing his confidence in this one fundamental aspect of his poetry.[2] He was aware that his genius lay embedded in the words and lines of his poetry, in his opening up "new potentialities of speech," and in developing for America a "cosmopolitan . . . range of self-expression." Like any poet, and especially a poet who experiments, Whitman wrote some bad lines and at times used language ineffectively. But more often than not, his lines were startlingly successful, and his language sparklingly individual and fresh and inevitable.[3]

It is difficult to define the quality that marks Whitman's language as his own and that was exactly suited to his themes of democracy and selfhood. But Emerson, in his 1855 letter, seemed to be pointing to this element when he said of the *Leaves,* "I find it the most extraordinary piece of wit and wisdom that America has yet contributed."[4] Whitman's wit inheres in his language; in his sometimes indiscriminate mixture of levels of usage; in his comic, occasionally grotesque use of foreign words and phrases; and in his blabbing, gabbing, and yawping in a multitude of mingled voices. His book is America's linguistic melting-pot; in it all the languages of all the people are mixed and stirred into one heady, hearty stew. His wisdom is folk-wisdom, which lives in the sayings of the people, in their chants, in their spells, in their incantations—in short, in their language. The essence of Whitman's wit and wisdom was suggested when he described, with relish and approval, the way in which slang invades language—like one of Shakespeare's clowns entering the "majestic audience-hall of the monarch."[5] Whitman frequently set the clown to juggling in the very middle of his majestic lines.

When Whitman wrote in "Song of Myself," "I know perfectly well my own egotism, / Know my omnivorous lines and must not write any less" (60), he was conducting one of his experiments with words. The connotations of the slightly bizarre *omnivorous* seem significantly applicable to the lines of the *Leaves*. There is not only a feeling of compul-

sion in the word but also the sense of all-inclusiveness for which the
poet's lines seem constantly struggling. But there is something omi-
nous or even sinister about *omnivorous* that also applies: it conveys the
feeling that the poet writes out of an obsession which is a wonder
mixed with terror, the terror of a man apart. The poet's lines devour
his energy, his flesh, his very soul—nothing is saved. His work thus
becomes the beast to which he flings himself in sacrifice, to which he
commits his personality, his very identity.

The image created by "omnivorous lines" is apt; for the dominant
impression one takes from *Leaves* is of lines *crammed* until there is room
for no more. This is, no doubt, an illusion that the poet intended to
create. Such an illusion could be evoked only by a multitude of concrete images (such as those in the catalogs) and not by a predominance
of abstractions. The individual line in Whitman tends, also, to be an
independent entity, complete in itself. This independence is especially
noticeable in the catalogs, where image follows image as line follows
line. Such independence is, perhaps, natural or even inevitable in lines
not confined by metrical pattern or rhyme. The following passage,
selected at random from that long, pivotal section in the middle of
"Song of Myself" (section 33), shows the self-sufficiency of each of the
lines in a catalog:

> Where the she-whale swims with her calf and never forsakes it,
> Where the steam-ship trails hind-ways its long pennant of smoke,
> Where the fin of the shark cuts like a black chip out of the
>   water,
>
>   (49)

Each of these lines constitutes a picture sharply focused and then
quickly dropped. Such a rapid flow of distinct and vivid scenes gives,
no doubt, just the effect Whitman desired of multiplicity, of teeming
life and endless diversity of objects. And each of these lines becomes a
challenge; for there is space for only the fewest of details by which
must be evoked a picture or scene: for the whale, it is her calf; for the
ship, its trail of smoke; for the shark, the fin cutting the water.

Frequently a line in Whitman seems to leap up from the page with
an independent life of its own, vibrant with a sharpness of detail, a
richness of metaphor, a fresh use of familiar words, a refreshing introduction of speech forms, or a novel or unusual combination of sounds.

One does not have to search far for examples. Indeed, in the case of Whitman, quantity itself has tended to become a dearth, for in the midst of so much the single item becomes submerged and is likely to pass unnoticed. The line unrooted from context and held under a special light no doubt suffers from loss of its natural habitat; but it gains, too, from a focus of attention that its setting tends to thwart. Such a line is that which closes section 41 of "Song of Myself": "Putting myself here and now to the ambush'd womb of the shadows" (59). That "ambush'd womb," startling image though it is, might very well be lost in the swiftly moving context. The poet, announcing that his day, the day of his fruition, is about to arrive, suggests by this striking image that he stands ready to seize the moment as his, no matter what time may give birth to. The uncertainty of the future is indicated by identifying this "ambush'd womb" as the "womb of the shadows." But the real ingenuity lies in the use of the word *ambush'd*. This word, juxtaposed to *womb*, inevitably connotes a potency (in the preceding line the poet has said that he is "becoming already a creator") of such force that it will not be denied its time of fulfillment.

Sometimes the brilliance of a line seems to derive almost solely from the simplicity of the detail. For example, "Leaving me baskets cover'd with white towels swelling the house with their plenty" (27). It would be difficult to settle on the significance of this line in context, but the details evoke a vivid, sharply drawn picture. And the transference of *swelling* from baskets to the house is curiously effective. Such a line as "Where the cattle stand and shake away flies with the tremulous shuddering of their hides" (49) evokes a static rural summer scene in which the only movement is that of cow's flesh twitching against the flies. In "I see the sparkles of starshine on the icy and pallid earth" (299), one views with the poet the round globe reflecting from its pale, glassy surface the glittering stars.

Frequently, however, the brilliance of a line lies in metaphor. There is an expression of supreme faith in, "I know I shall not pass like a child's carlacue cut with a burnt stick at night" (38). The *carlacue*, whose meaningless, whimsical abstraction glows briefly in the night, signifies life as it would appear were there no purpose pervading the universe. "The damp of the night drives deeper into my soul" (46) uses a vivid, visual, and sensuous image to describe the poet's somber emotional state. The dominant, driving *d*'s underscore the depth of the feeling. The entire line, "From your formules, O bat-eyed and mater-

ialistic priests" (112), seems to explode with *bat-eyed*; the staring but
unseeing priests, enamored with *things,* materialize before us gravely
solemn.

In "Always these compact lands tied at the hips with the belt string-
ing the huge oval lakes" (125), the poet demonstrates his genius in
bringing landscapes to warm life; one sees not merely a human image,
but a man, perhaps a vagabond, jauntily striding the open road—the
personified cocky spirit of "these compact lands." In "For it [science]
has history gather'd like husks around the globe" (166), the crust of
the earth, compacted history, becomes a shell to be opened and ana-
lyzed. In "Through angers, losses, ambition, ignorance, ennui, what
you are picks its way" (172), the series of abstractions is suddenly
brought up short against the image of an individual carefully finding
his footing amidst a multitude of concrete hazards. Immense and turbulent grief is ascribed to the sea in such a short line as, "The white
arms out in the breakers tirelessly tossing" (181). With "I am a
dance—play up there! the fit is whirling me fast!" (298), the poet
transforms himself into the essence of rhythmical movement, and the
reader finds himself confronted with the blur of the rapid whirl.

A measure of the poet's achievement in the use of vivid metaphor
may be taken by examination of a series of lines that describe the successive emotional states of the poet as he is "whirl[ed]" by an orchestra
which "wrenches such ardors" from him:

> It sails me, I dab with bare feet, they are lick'd by the
>   indolent waves,
> I am cut by bitter and angry hail, I lose my breath,
> Steep'd amid honey'd morphine, my windpipe throttled in
>   fakes of death,
> At length let up again . . .
>
>   (44–45)

This rich imagery ranges from the extremes of the peaceful to the violent. First the poet is "sailed" by the music, a sensation made meaningful by another, and extraordinary, metaphor—"bare feet . . . lick'd
by the indolent waves." Such a feeling of sensual ecstasy is transformed
suddenly into a feeling of violent fear, conveyed through the image of
the hostile hail, suggesting that even this signature of the universe has
made the poet an outcast. But next the agitation disappears; there
comes in its place a quiet which, at first peaceful, suddenly seems near

the stasis of death. "Steep'd amid honey'd morphine" evokes the very essence of drugged immobility and suggests an imminent disengagement with life. Even breathing seems cut off in imitation of death. Then, "at length," the poet is "let up again"—an indication that he was *possessed* by the music and made to conform emotionally to its every whim and will.

If many of Whitman's lines seem to succeed through the very simplicity of the detail or metaphor, others seem to succeed through the fusion of a series of related details. For example, "The blab of the pave, tires of the carts, sluff of boot-soles, talk of the promenaders" (30) is unsurpassable in evoking, in the fewest possible words, the hectic chaos of a busy street scene. All of these images of sound merge into the indistinguishable "blab of the pave." In such a line as "The prostitute draggles her shawl, her bonnet bobs on her tipsy and pimpled neck" (35), the details of the shawl, bonnet, and neck merge to create a vivid picture of a slightly ludicrous, slightly repulsive streetwalker. Two metaphors combined with simple details in "Behaviour lawless as snow-flakes, words simple as grass, uncomb'd head, laughter, and naivetè" (56) create an impression of an individual filled with a freedom as wild as it is refreshing. The freedom is the primitive freedom of nature itself. In such a line as "To dance, clap hands, exult, shout, leap, roll on, float on" (134), detail is piled on detail to evoke a vivid impression of frenetic movement that finally achieves its release from gravity. In "The shape of the sly settee, and the adulterous unwholesome couple" (142), the two details are sufficient to suggest an entire world of guilt and deceit.

Frequently the effect in Whitman's line derives from a distortion of language, or from incongruous combinations whose very incongruity offers fresh insight. Sometimes the poet's ear betrays him. Some of his borrowings, particularly from the French (for example, *ma femme* and *feuillage*), seem not just mistakes of the ear but grotesque misjudgment. But, on the other hand, had the poet not attempted these, he probably would not have struck off such an ingenious concoction as "No dainty dolce affettuoso, I, / Bearded, sunburnt, gray-neck'd, forbidding I have arrived" (22). One need not be bothered much about the meaning of "dolce affettuoso"—its look on the page and its sound are enough to justify it a hundredfold. But there are other eccentric uses of language. In "Earth of the slumbering and liquid trees!" (39), one is hard put to explain the meaning of "slumbering and liquid." The *slumbering* may be a simple transference from the people to the trees, but the *liquid,* even though one instinctively recognizes its rightness, is not so simple to explain. Since this is an "earth of departed sunset," the massed trees at night perhaps give the impression of a body of water, their movement in the wind suggesting the movement of waves. But, too, there is no doubt significance in the use of *liquid* in a passage which is only superficially descriptive and is primarily sexually suggestive.

There is an elusive quality in a good many lines in *Leaves,* which, though hard to define, nevertheless constitutes the effect: "Who goes there? hankering, gross, mystical, nude; / How is it I extract strength from the beef I eat?" (38). The next question the poet asks ("What is a man anyhow?") indicates sufficiently the sense in these two lines, but it does not reveal the secret of their curious success. There is something of a clash of language in the use of *mystical* amid *hankering, gross,* and *nude.* And it is perhaps in this clash, in this tension between the two extremes of *mystical* and *gross,* that the desired effect is achieved. The pondering of the philosophical question as to what is man, alongside the contemplation of physical man, "gross," "nude," eating beef and extracting strength, results in the kind of paradox (the spiritual inseparable from the material) in which the poet delighted and with which he wished to startle his readers into perception. This incongruity in language results in a gravely irreverent, nonchalantly serious tone. Whitman is not joking; but neither is he speaking with ponderous gravity. This tone, Whitman's distinguishing mark, is present frequently throughout *Leaves of Grass.* It is present in "The spotted hawk swoops by and accuses me, he complains of my gab and my loitering," and in "I sound my barbaric yawp over the roofs of the world" (68). It is injected in the first instance by *gab,* in the second by *yawp,* words that gather the lines to a focus. And this tone is sounded loudly in "Earth! you seem to look for something at my hands, / Say, old top-knot, what do you want?" (57). The *top-knot* has just the right ring to bring the earth down to a level of intimate familiarity with the poet. The language—easy, colloquial, salty—is that of a man to his boon companion and equal. Such is the language of the title of the final poem in *Leaves of Grass,* "So Long—" hardly the formal farewell one would expect on an occasion of such solemnity.

This "irreverent" tone becomes the whole basis for "Song of the Exposition," in which the invocation to the muse is made in a chatty and intimate style:

> Come Muse migrate from Greece and Ionia,
> Cross out please those immensely overpaid accounts,

That matter of Troy and Achilles' wrath, and Aeneas',
    Odysseus' wanderings,
Placard "Removed" and "To Let" on the rocks of your
    snowy Parnassus,

(143)

The tone is irreverent and the manner familiar—the tone and manner
of a vigorous, self-reliant young man addressing a somewhat dowdy
goddess of diminished divinity—a goddess who must transfigure
herself into a domestic democrat. When the advice is taken and
the lady (now the "illustrious emigré") strides onto the scene, "vigor-
ously clearing a path," the poet announces (as in the ballyhoo of a
circus):

By thud of machinery and shrill steam-whistle undismay'd,
Bluff'd not a bit by drain-pipe, gasometers, artificial
    fertilizers,
Smiling and pleas'd with palpable intent to stay,
She's here, install'd amid the kitchen ware!

(144)

This environment for Whitman's muse seems entirely appropriate.
The irreverence of surrounding the dignified Old World muse with
drainpipes, artificial fertilizers and kitchenware is the irreverence of a
self-assured, democratic, supremely individualistic young poet. And
the effect is achieved through a blending of the mystical with the natural, the elevated with the lowly, the spiritual with the physical. The
muse amidst the kitchenware is the apt symbol for Whitman's wit. It
is the quality that is the essence of the line, "To be wrestled with as I
pass for the solid prizes of the universe" (22), and that prevades "I am
he who tauntingly compels men, women, nations, / Crying, Leap from
your seats and contend for your lives!" (242).

But with all his careful attention to, and blending of, levels of usage
in language, Whitman also has a careful ear attuned to the melody of
the sounds of words. No man who wrote "Down-hearted doubters dull
and excluded" (61) could have been oblivious to harmony in word
sounds. How much, for example, of the effect of "Only the lull I like,
the hum of your valvèd voice" (27) derives from the repeated *l*'s and
v's, balancing the two halves of the line rhythmically. Something of
Whitman's attitude is revealed in "Starting from Paumanok":

The red aborigines,
Leaving natural breaths, sounds of rain and winds, calls
        as of birds and animals in the woods, syllabled to
        us for names,
Okonee, Koosa, Ottawa, Monongahela, Sauk, Natchez,
        Chattahoochee, Kaqueta, Oronoco,
Wabash, Miami, Saginaw, Chippewa, Oshkosh, Walla-Walla,
Leaving such to the states they melt, they depart, charging
        the water and the land with names.

                                                    (23)

The ear that heard the music, and not only music, but "natural breaths, sounds of rain and winds" in these Indian names could not have been deaf to the sounds of words. Two entire lines are devoted merely to the repetition of this "syllabled" nature. And as the tribes disappear, the names they leave in their stead *charge* "the water and the land," bringing them to vibrant life. This unseen life is "what the air holds of the red aborigines." In a poem in "Sands at Seventy," Whitman exploits the music and connotations inherent in a name— "Yonnondio":

        A song, a poem of itself—the word itself a dirge,
        Amid the wilds, the rocks, the storm and wintry night,
        To me such misty, strange tableaux the syllables calling
                up;

                                                    (361)

The vision of the red people emerges, then fades, all at the instance of the sound of the word "Yonnondio": "A muffled sonorous sound, a wailing word is borne through the air for a moment, / Then blank and gone and still, and utterly lost" (361).

    A climax in word magic or incantation is reached in one of the most curious poems in *Leaves*, "Unfolded Out of the Folds," in which the poet fully exploits both sound and meaning:

        Unfolded out of the folds of the woman man comes unfolded,
                and is always to come unfolded,
        Unfolded only out of the superbest woman of the earth is to
                come the superbest man of the earth,

> Unfolded out of the friendliest woman is to come the
>   friendliest man,
>
>   (276)

Complexity of meaning is introduced in succeeding lines:

> Unfolded by brawny embraces from the well-muscled woman
>   I love, only thence come the brawny embraces of the man.
> Unfolded out of the folds of the woman's brain come all the
>   folds of the man's brain, duly obedient,
>
>   (276)

The imagery that flashes through the hypnotic sound delineates the two sides of man's nature, his physical and spiritual, or sexual and intellectual—both derived from woman. This poem elevates woman to the very highest position, attributing all that man is to her; and the poet asserts, in characteristic language, "every jot of the greatness of man is unfolded out of woman," the *every jot* underscoring a jaunty certainty. The poem concludes: "First the man is shaped in the woman, he can then be shaped in himself" (276). The small word *in* gathers each half of this verse into sharp focus, its shift in meaning creating the poetic life of the line. "Unfolded Out of the Folds" shows Whitman, through the magic of his incantation, coming to linguistic terms with his omnivorous lines.

Chapter Eight
The Bardic Voice

Each generation has created Whitman in its own image. As he is a poet who contains multitudes, it is not difficult to find in him diverse and conflicting philosophies and attitudes. He has been called the poet of the family, and he has been called the poet of free love. He has been labeled poet of democracy, and he has been claimed by socialists and communists. He has been proclaimed poet of science, and he has been hailed as the poet of mysticism. He has been criticized as provincially patriotic, and he has been censured for indiscriminately embracing the world's masses. No doubt a part of Whitman's greatness lies in his multifaceted appeal. As long as we do not mistake a part for the whole, it is valuable to isolate and examine single aspects of his work. No comprehensive treatment of the poet may properly ignore two strong and central elements in his work—sexual energy and mysticism. Nor should his claims as America's archetypal and epic poet be too quickly brushed aside. And some reconsideration needs to be given to the living literary tradition with which he is deeply allied.

Sexual Energy and Life Force

"[Henry] Adams began to ponder, asking himself whether he knew of any American artist who had ever insisted on the power of sex, as every classic had always done; but he could think only of Walt Whitman. . . . All the rest had used sex for sentiment, never for force."[1] Thus wrote Adams about himself in *The Education of Henry Adams.* Many prudish and righteous readers have been so shocked and outraged by the sex themes in the *Leaves* that they have been blinded to their real meaning and significance. The self-appointed censors who wanted to tamper with the *Leaves* would gladly have castrated it to render it "clean." They never realized how pervasive and vital to the lifeblood of the book was the procreational element. Whitman knew. He wrote in "A Backward Glance O'er Travel'd Roads," "*Leaves of Grass* is avowedly the song of Sex. . . . The espousing principle of those lines so gives breath of life to my whole scheme that the bulk of the pieces might as

well have been left unwritten were those lines omitted. . . . The lines
I allude to, and the spirit in which they are spoken, permeate all *Leaves
of Grass,* and the work must stand or fall with them" (452).

From one point of view the earlier pages of *Leaves* present a kind of
sexual biography, a dramatization of the successive states of sexual con-
sciousnesses of the poetic hero. In "Song of Myself" the poet achieves
intense self-awareness only through sexual awakening:

> Is this then a touch? quivering me to a new identity,
> Flames and ether making a rush for my veins,
> Treacherous tip of me reaching and crowding to help them,
> My flesh and blood playing out lightning to strike what is
>   hardly different from myself,
> On all sides prurient provokers stiffening my limbs,
> Straining the udder of my heart for its withheld drip,
>
>   (45)

The entire passage devoted to "blind loving wrestling touch" is ego-
centric, a sexual experience in which the isolated self is inwardly absorbed in the discovery of new intensities and levels of feeling.

In "Children of Adam" the consciousness projects outward from the
self to embrace a partner. Announcing his intention to sing the song
of the phallus and procreation, the poet celebrates "The mystic deliria,
the madness amorous, the utter abandonment" (70). No longer is the
poet alone; he becomes Adam with his Eve:

> I draw you close to me, you women,
> I cannot let you go, I would do you good,
> I am for you, and you are for me, not only for our own
>   sake, but for others' sakes,
> Envelop'd in you sleep greater heroes and bards,
> They refuse to awake at the touch of any man but me.
>
>   (77)

The sexual consciousness is not only extended to another individual,
but the center of feeling is shifted to the procreational aspects of the
experience. No longer driven backward on itself, the sexual identity
extends outward to woman, and on beyond into the future: "I shall
look for loving crops from the birth, life, death, immortality, I plant
so lovingly now" (78).

In "Calamus" the poet's sexual consciousness extends beyond the female to celebrate "manly attachment," "types of athletic love," the "need of comrades" (84). Just as in "Children of Adam" the poet's sexual imagination extends beyond the immediate experience to the "loving crops" to come, so in "Calamus" his "adhesive" imagination soars beyond the specific attachment to the race of "magnetic lands": "I will plant companionship thick as trees along all the rivers of America, and along the shores of the great lakes, and all over the prairies, / I will make inseparable cities with their arms about each other's necks" (87). In one poem Whitman juxtaposed the two kinds of love, man-woman and man-man, in order to dramatize the difference:

> Fast-anchor'd eternal O love! O woman I love!
> O bride! O wife! more resistless than I can tell, the
>   thought of you!
> Then separate, as disembodied or another born,
> Ethereal, the last athletic reality, my consolation,
> I ascend, I float in the regions of your love O man,
> O sharer of my roving life.
>
>   (98)

The phallic symbolism and the overtones of romantic love in "Calamus" are inescapable. But so too is the poet's constant, sometimes dramatically anguished attempt to transfigure the adhesive attachment into pure spirituality, art, and democracy: "Not in any or all of them O adhesiveness! O pulse of my life! / Need I that you exist and show yourself any more than in these songs" (88); "I loved a certain person ardently and my love was not return'd, / Yet out of that I have written these songs" (97).

The reader who wishes may reduce "Song of Myself," "Children of Adam," and "Calamus" to mere auto-, hetero,- or homoerotic impulse. He does so, however, by ignoring their complexity of vision and their validity and intensity of feeling. In sex as in other facets of life, Whitman made a universal embrace, taking to himself the whole range of sexual feeling and emotion. He anticipated the modern psychologies which have affirmed that these feelings are familiar to the individual at one time or another in the development from child to adult. At a time when Victorian gentility, its finger to its lips, shunned any talk of man's "lower" nature, Whitman insisted on acceptance and celebration of human sexual nature in all its manifestations and complexity. It was this element in his poetry that made Whitman (as D. H. Lawrence was to say)[2] a great beginner and pioneer.

But Whitman's sexual imagery is not confined to the limits of the human drama. As he insisted, it "permeates" all the *Leaves*.[3] Just as his procreative poetry is not primarily a love poetry, but a poetry of sexual energy, so his sexual images recur throughout his work deeply implicated in the cosmic drama. Through sexual imagery Whitman identifies the person with the fundamental generative forces in nature. In sexual identity and experience the person may discover harmony and unity with nature, the life-force that subterraneously unites all into one creative whole.

Whitman's sexual vision transfigures the very landscape he looks upon: "Sprouts take and accumulate, stand by the curb prolific and vital, / Landscapes projected masculine, full-sized and golden" (46). His vision extends to the heavens:

> Hefts of the moving world at innocent gambols silently
>   rising, freshly exuding,
> Scooting obliquely high and low.
>
> Something I cannot see puts upward libidinous prongs,
> Seas of bright juice suffuse heaven.
>
>   (43)

And his sexual imagination plays through all of the natural world:

> Root of wash'd sweet-flag! timorous pond-snipe! nest of
>   guarded duplicate eggs! it shall be you!
> Mix'd tussled hay of head, beard, brawn, it shall be you!
> Trickling sap of maple, fibre of manly wheat, it shall be you!
> Sun so generous it shall be you!
> Vapors lighting and shading my face it shall be you!
> You sweaty brooks and dews it shall be you!
> Winds whose soft-tickling genitals rub against me it shall
>   be you!
>
>   (42)

Some of the most moving of Whitman's sexual passages are in reality dramatic vignettes of cosmic forces in rhythmical, generative union. Such is the striking passage in "Children of Adam"—"Bridegroom night of love working surely and softly into the prostrate dawn" (73). Such too is one of the most brilliant passages in "Song of Myself":

I am he that walks with the tender and growing night,
I call to the earth and sea half-held by the night.

Press close bare-bosom'd night—press close magnetic
    nourishing night!
Night of south winds—night of the large few stars!
Still nodding night—mad naked summer night.

Smile O voluptuous cool-breath'd earth!
Earth of the slumbering and liquid trees!
Earth of departed sunset—earth of the mountains
    misty-topt!
Earth of the vitreous pour of the full moon just
    tinged with blue!
Earth of shine and dark mottling the tide of the river!
Earth of the limpid gray of clouds brighter and clearer
    for my sake!
Far-swooping elbow'd earth—rich apple-blossom'd earth!
Smile, for your lover comes.

                                                    (39)

In this passage all of nature enters into the sexual drama with passionate intensity. Even the sea extends its "crooked inviting fingers," and
dashes with its "amorous wet." Encompassing the earth and the heavens, pervading the night and the sea, the poet's sexual vision penetrates
the surface of nature to the pulsating force that vitalizes all.

In its ultimate meaning, then, the poet's sexual vision connects with
his mystic vision, for the first leads to the universal identification that
the second assumes in achieving spiritual union. In "We Two, How
Long We Were Fool'd," the two are transported to new identities by
their experience:

Now transmuted, we swiftly escape as Nature escapes,
We are Nature, long have we been absent, but now we return,
We become plants, trunks, foliage, roots, bark,
We are bedded in the ground, we are rocks,
We are oaks, we grow in the openings side by side,
We browse, we are two among the wild herds spontaneous
    as any,

                                                    (81)

The themes of sexual energy and identification in *Leaves* extend far
beyond the conventional themes of romantic love literature; they lie at
the very heart of Whitman's profoundest cosmic meanings.

Mysticism

Although Whitman is one of the most physical of poets, although he repeatedly celebrates the body and sex, he is also one of the most mystical, proclaiming as one of his major themes the soul and its destiny. He takes seriously the principle announced in his 1855 Preface, that readers rightfully expect the poet to "indicate the path between reality and their souls" (415). In "Song of Myself" he announced:

> I am the poet of the Body and I am the poet of the Soul,
> The pleasures of heaven are with me and the pains of hell
>   are with me,
> The first I graft and increase upon myself, the latter I
>   translate into a new tongue.
>
>   (39)

In elevating the body with the soul, in "translating" the "pains of hell" into a "new tongue," Whitman departs markedly from the traditional mystic. Indeed, there is in Whitman far too much assertion of self (as in "Song of Myself") and far too much wanderlust and involvement (as in "Song of the Open Road") to identify him explicitly with either Christian or Oriental mysticism. But the mystical elements dramatized in his poetry extend down into his deepest meanings.

The vital relationship of the body to the mystical experience and the identification of the "mystic deliria" as analogous with it are both strongly suggested in the key section 5 of "Song of Myself," in which the poet appears to be going into the mystic trance:

> Loafe with me on the grass, loose the stop from your throat,
> Not words, not music or rhyme I want, not custom or lecture,
>   not even the best,
> Only the lull I like, the hum of your valvèd voice.
>
> I mind how once we lay such a transparent summer morning,
> How you settled your head athwart my hips and gently turn'd
>   over upon me,
> And parted the shirt from my bosom-bone, and plunged
>   your tongue to my bare-stript heart,
> And reach'd till you felt my beard, and reach'd till you held
>   my feet.
>
>   (27–28)

The sexual imagery is unmistakable. In another context the passage might well appear to be a physical drama of ecstatic sexual experience. But in its own context, it is a mystic interfusion of body and soul. The poet has just asserted "I believe in you my soul, the other I am must not abase itself to you, / And you must not be abased to the other" (27). The passage that comes after is a passionate love scene, but the participants are the body and soul, the soul playing the role of the aggressor probing the poet's inmost privacy, seizing and caressing with the intimate abandon of a lover.

At this high moment of feeling, when the body has been invaded and held helplessly captive by the soul, the poet achieves transcendent illumination:

> Swiftly arose and spread around me the peace and knowledge
>   that pass all the argument of the earth,
> And I know that the hand of God is the promise of my own,
> And I know that the spirit of God is the brother of my own,
> And that all the men ever born are also my brothers, and the
>   women my sisters and lovers,
> And that a kelson of the creation is love,
>
>   (28)

Mystics have always asserted that the knowledge bestowed by their experience passes "all the argument of the earth." Theirs is an intuitive knowledge that originates not in the logic of the mind but in the spontaneity of the soul.

Further exploration of "Song of Myself" (see chapter 5) reveals many striking parallels with the mystical experience. In his *The Varieties of Religious Experience,* William James defined mysticism as a state of consciousness characterized by two qualities: *noetic,* a state of transcendent, nonintellectual insight and revelation; and *ineffable,* inexpressible in ordinary human language, known only through the experience itself.[4] These qualities abound, not only in "Song of Myself," but throughout the *Leaves.* In "Inscriptions" Whitman writes: "I myself but write one or two indicative words for the future, / I but advance a moment only to wheel and hurry back in the darkness" (13). Whitman asserts repeatedly throughout *Leaves* that his words are inadequate, that the reader must make his own discoveries through his own experiences.

One quality of all mysticism, whether Christian, secular, or Oriental, is its apprehension of unity pervading all the universe. Mystics frequently attempt to explain their experience as some kind of merge or Union with an Other which is All. Whitman's poetry tends constantly in this direction, proceeding from diversity to unity. His endless catalogs, which sometimes seem indiscriminate inventories of the things in the world, always move toward some kind of unity, either in the poet's imagination or in the spiritual world it constructs. "Crossing Brooklyn Ferry" derives its main impulse from this point of view; all the "dumb, beautiful ministers" of the poem—the river, the "scallop-edg'd waves," the clouds, the "masts of Mannahatta," the "beautiful hills of Brooklyn," and more—are transfigured into spiritual unity within the beholders of all ages, and flow into the grand spiritual Union of All: "we plant you permanently within us, / . . . You furnish your parts toward eternity, / Great or small, you furnish your parts toward the soul" (120).

But it is in "Passage to India" that Whitman's mysticism most clearly stresses Union. From the physical or material union of the world achieved by the engineers, the poem moves swiftly and surely to the spiritual Union that is the province of mysticism. The poet calls to his soul to venture further and further, to transcend the barriers of time and space:

> O soul thou pleasest me, I thee,
> Sailing these seas or on the hills, or waking in the night,
> Thoughts, silent thoughts, of Time and Space and Death,
>   like waters flowing,
> Bear me indeed as through the regions infinite,
> Whose air I breathe, whose ripples hear, lave me all over,
> Bathe me O God in thee, mounting to thee,
> I and my soul to range in range of thee.
>
> (293)

At this point of mystic merge, the poet attempts to name the "Nameless"—"transcendent," "the fibre and the breath," "light of the light, shedding forth universes"—but always one metaphor is abandoned in its inadequacy for another. In turning his thoughts to himself, the poet is more successful in conveying the sense of Union, the mingling of the self with the All:

> Swiftly I shrivel at the thought of God,
> At Nature and its wonders, Time and Space and Death,

But that I, turning, call to thee O soul, thou actual Me,
And lo, thou gently masterest the orbs,
Thou matest Time, smilest content at Death,
And fillest, swellest full the vastnesses of Space.

(293)

By its endless extension into eternity and by its unlimited expansion
into infinity, the poet's soul apprehends directly the Union sought by
all the mystics throughout all lands and ages.

It is perhaps easiest to trace Whitman's mysticism to Emersonian
transcendentalism, and to envision Whitman as merely fulfilling
Emerson's doctrine of self-trust, the doctrine asserting that every man
should commune with the divinity (or the animating oversoul) within
himself. And there can be no doubt that in the mystical insights of his
poems Whitman resembles the ideal American scholar described by
Emerson: "In self-trust all the virtues are comprehended. Free should
the scholar be,—free and brave."[5] (In his famed 1855 letter to Whitman, Emerson used precisely these words: "I give you joy of your free
and brave thought.") Emerson recognized what he had been calling
for, but he also knew that Whitman's poetry was no mere parroting of
transcendental doctrine; he confessed that he found it "the most extraordinary piece of wit and wisdom that America has yet contributed."
Thoreau, too, found more than mere imitation transcendentalism in
Whitman; he found him so "wonderfully like the Orientals" that he
asked Whitman if he had read them, to which Whitman replied, "No:
tell me about them."[6]

From the very beginning Whitman's critics attempted to define the
intangible mystical element in the *Leaves*. In *The Good Gray Poet*
(1866), W. D. O'Connor detected a "sacerdotal and prophetic character
which makes it a sort of American Bible."[7] In *Notes on Walt Whitman
as Poet and Person* (1867, revised 1871), John Burroughs spoke of the
"long train of revelations" which made *Leaves* "like the bibles of nations."[8] But it was Richard M. Bucke, the Canadian psychiatrist, who
first tried to describe with some precision the essential distinctiveness
of Whitman's mysticism. Bucke's book, *Cosmic Consciousness* (1901),
expounded a theory of three levels of consciousness: Simple, Self, and
Cosmic, the first an attribute of animals, the second of man, and the
third of the rare human who is prophet, seer, mystic—including Gua-
tama the Buddha, Jesus the Christ, and Walt Whitman (among

others).[9] In *Varieties of Religious Experience* (1902), William James tried to do in a scholarly way what Bucke had done intuitively. James cited Whitman as an example of the "sporadic type of mystical experience."[10] Both Bucke and James seemed to accept the notion of some specific spiritual experience in Whitman's life underlying the mystical elements in his poetry.

Whatever the origin of the mysticism in Whitman, it seems clear that his most dynamic connections run more deeply than merely to Emersonian transcendentalism or even to Wordsworthian romanticism. He goes back in a vital way to a prophetic poet like Blake, whom he did not know; or he looks forward to a prophetic philosopher like Nietzsche, whom he could not have read. Although it is difficult at first glance to reconcile Whitman's mysticism with his strong materialism, his assertion of self, his restless vagabondage, and his celebrated sexuality, the mystical theme asserts itself in *Leaves* by its sheer power and vitality. In the last analysis, Whitman's temperament seems eminently unsuited to the selflessness of the Christian mystic and to the passivity of the Oriental. He is far too much bound up in his own consciousness and selfhood and far too fully committed to wandering the open road. It is possible that Whitman, out of the multiple obscure sources and out of his own soul, created a unique mysticism designed for America—a "democratic" mysticism available to every person on equal terms, embracing both body and soul, science and myth, life and death, active and passive, material and spiritual. But whatever the ultimate nature of his mysticism, it must be granted a central role in the meaning of his greatest poetry in *Leaves*.

Epic

When W. D. O'Connor and John Burroughs spoke of *Leaves of Grass* as a kind of American Bible, they were attempting to identify an aspect of the work that Whitman thought its most important. Not, however, that Whitman tried to found a New World religion; rather, he tried to provide a great archetypal work of literature suitable for the new civilization of America.

Whitman did not reject the masterpieces of the past. He said in "A Backward Glance": "The New World receives with joy the poems of the antique, with European feudalism's rich fund of epics, plays, ballads—seeks not in the least to deaden or displace those voices from our ear and area—holds them indeed as indispensable studies, influences, records, comparisons" (448). Whitman is careful to pay tribute to the "precious bequest" of the "old songs ferried hither from east and west." But he poses the crucial question: "Of the great poems receiv'd from abroad and from the ages, and to-day enveloping and penetrating America, is there one that is consistent with these United States, or essentially applicable to them as they are and are to be?" (448). The old bibles and epics, the great archetypal poems of the past, were great for their day and provide a rich fund for the present, but can they substitute for a great native literature?

The answer is, of course, *no*. And Whitman's hope for the *Leaves* was that they would become for America what the great epic poems of the past became for the civilizations they embodied and idealized ("A Backward Glance"): "As America fully and fairly construed is the legitimate result and evolutionary outcome of the past, so I would dare to claim for my verse. Without stopping to qualify the averment, the Old World has had the poems of myths, fictions, feudalism, conquest, caste, dynastic wars, and splendid exceptional characters and affairs, which have been great; but the New World needs the poems of realities and science and of the democratic average and basic equality, which shall be greater. In the centre of all, and object of all, stands the Human Being, towards whose heroic and spiritual evolution poems and everything directly or indirectly tend, Old World or New" (449).

In short, Whitman intended the *Leaves* to serve as America's epic. There is every indication of such an intent at the very beginning of the *Leaves*—Whitman announces his themes and invokes the muse after the fashion of the epic: "Of Life immense in passion, pulse, and power, / Cheerful, for freest action form'd under the laws divine, / The Modern Man I sing" (5). In this opening poem, Whitman insists on his themes of democracy and modernity so openly that, in the second poem, he arouses the Old World Muse: "A Phantom arose before me with distrustful aspect, / Terrible in beauty, age, and power, / The genius of poets of old lands" (5). The Muse informs the poet that the only theme possible for "ever-enduring bards" is the theme of War—"the fortune of battles," "the making of perfect soldiers." And the poet answers that these are precisely his themes: his war has for its field the world, and it is fought for "life and death, for the Body and for the eternal Soul." And he concludes, "I above all promote brave soldiers" (6).

The Muse appears again in the *Leaves,* receiving something like her Americanization in "Song of the Exposition." At the direct invitation of the poet, she departs her hallowed haunts abroad and migrates to the New World:

> The dame of dames! can I believe then,
> Those ancient temples, sculptures classic, could none of
>   them retain her?
> Nor shades of Virgil and Dante, nor myriad memories,
>   poems, old associations, magnetize and hold on to her?
> But that she's left them all—and here?
>
> (143–44)

The "illustrious emigré" is "here" indeed, and she is democratically installed "amid the kitchen ware!" The poet turns the tables and offers his courage to the Muse:

> Fear not O Muse! truly new ways and days received,
>   surround you,
> I candidly confess a queer, queer race, of novel fashion,
> And yet the same old human race, the same within, without,
> Faces and hearts the same, feelings the same, yearnings
>   the same,
> The same old love, beauty and use the same.
>
> (145)

Although the tone throughout in the treatment of this slightly puzzled Muse is gently humorous, the insistence on native poetic themes is serious. But, even though the themes seem new, it is still the "same old human race."

This somewhat diminished Muse gives way again to the earlier Phantom in "By Blue Ontario's Shore." In this poem the Muse, already thoroughly American, is making demands on the poet for a native song:

> A Phantom gigantic superb, with stern visage accosts me,
> *Chant me the poem,* it said, *that comes from the soul of*
>   *America, chant me the carol of victory,*
> *And strike up the marches of Libertad, marches more*
>   *powerful yet,*
> *And sing me before you go the song of the throes of*
>   *Democracy.*
>
> (241)

The poet launches into his long chant on these themes, and he turns ultimately to calling forth a race of American bards: "I listened to the Phantom by Ontario's shore, / I heard the voice arising demanding bards" (245). These cards are to be a kind of capstone to the American idea and image: "By them all native and grand, by them alone can these States be fused into the compact organism of a Nation" (245). Before Whitman has advanced far in his outline of the American bard, he confesses that his own *Leaves* fit the pattern:

> Fall behind me States!
> A man before all—myself, typical, before all.
>
> Give me the pay I have served for,
> Give me to sing the songs of the great Idea, take all the rest,
> I have loved the earth, sun, animals, I have despised riches,
>   (249)

In his concentration on himself as "typical," in his insistence on "individuals" above and "underneath all," the poet is prepared to present himself as the epic New World hero: "America isolated yet embodying all, what is it finally except myself? / These States, what are they except myself?" (251). The "Modern Man" Whitman announces as his theme in the opening poem of the *Leaves* is none other than himself.

Central to all national epics is the epic hero embodying the personal ideals of a civilization and a culture. When Whitman reviewed in "A Backward Glance" the motivating impulse that originated the *Leaves,* he defined the desire that "dominated everything else": "This was a feeling or ambition to articulate and faithfully express in literary or poetic form, and uncompromisingly, my own physical, emotional, moral, intellectual, and aesthetic Personality, in the midst of, and tallying, the momentous spirit and facts of its immediate days, and of current America—and to exploit that Personality, identified with place and date, in a far more candid and comprehensive sense than any hitherto poem or book" (444).

In exploiting himself, Whitman transcended himself. The "I" in *Leaves* is never simply the historical Walter Whitman; but it always embraces him and goes on beyond to the ideal. Whitman did not transcribe himself so much as *dramatize* the various images he created of his Personality. He is his own epic hero, but he emerges from *Leaves* as clearly mythical as Homer's or Virgil's heroes. He emerges larger than life, displaying traits of Democracy's Superman.

In short, the Walt of the *Leaves* is the archetypal epic hero for American Democracy. Whenever he magnifies himself, he takes along the reader: "And what I assume you shall assume, / For every atom belonging to me as good belongs to you" (25). He sternly warns his reader: "Not I, not any one else can travel that road for you, / You must travel it for yourself" (64). If *Leaves* embodies the ideal, it is an ideal placed within the grasps of all who aspire to it. This is no hero endowed with divine characteristics beyond the reach of the mass of men: his divine characteristics are the common right of each individual who breathes and sees and feels—and awakens himself to his own humanness. Each man may become his own hero.

If *Leaves* is America's epic, what is the myth it embodies and preserves? We are perhaps too close to the nineteenth century to say. But Whitman suggested the answer when he wrote of his original intentions in "A Backward Glance": "Plenty of songs had been sung—beautiful, matchless songs—adjusted to other lands than these—another spirit and stage of evolution; but I would sing, and leave out or put in, quite solely with reference to America and to-day. Modern science and democracy seem'd to be throwing out their challenge to poetry to put them in its statements in contradistinction to the songs and myths of the past" (444). This statement constitutes a kind of confession that *science* and *democracy* assume the role of myth in the *Leaves*. In a sense, they do become a substitute for the religion and the gods of past epics; they fill the vacuum created by the modern age's loss of belief and faith. When (in "Song of Myself") Whitman shouts, "Hurrah for positive science! long live exact demonstration!" (41) or chants with awe (in "Song of the Broad-Axe"), "Her shape arises, / She less guarded than ever, yet more guarded than ever" (142), he seems to be trying to transfigure his *science* and *democracy* into deities, to elevate them to the level of gods.

In musing over his response to the "challenge" of nineteenth-century America's myth—science and democracy—Whitman commented: "As I see it now (perhaps too late,) I have unwittingly taken up that challenge and made an attempt at such statements—which I certainly would not assume to do now, knowing more clearly what it means" (444–45). Here the poet seems dangerously close to confessing his own loss of faith. More likely, he is seeing clearly for the first time, in the "candlelight" of his old age, the stupendous size of the task he had brashly set out to accomplish in his youth. And perhaps he is realizing in retrospect that the science and democracy of his culture and age

that he embraced so warmly as absolute truths have no more fundamental validity than the myths of the older classics or of epics yet to
be sung.

The Bardic Tradition

Although the *Leaves* has been read now for over a century, there is
still uncertainty about its genuine alliances. The tendency has been to
place Whitman as the forerunner of poets like Edgar Lee Masters,
Vachel Lindsay, and Carl Sandburg. And there are superficial resemblances between Whitman's democratic voice and Masters's multitude
of small-town voices, between Whitman's frenzied accumulations and
the calculated chants of Lindsay, between Whitman's yawping rugged-
ness and the sprawling prolixity of Sandburg. But these connections
play primarily on the surface; they do not run deep. By linking Whitman with these secondary figures of twentieth-century poetry, friendly
critics have unintentionally shunted him off on a side track; and hostile
critics have delightedly agreed that his influences have played themselves out on imaginations generally unrelated to the central poetic
currents of the age.

The dominant poetic influences of the twentieth century, Ezra
Pound and T. S. Eliot, have been powerful in their condemnation of
Whitman. Pound's flip comment in *ABC of Reading* that, when he
returned to Whitman after a period of years, he could not find the
thirty well-written pages he once had thought were there, is typical of
the casual literary dismissal of Whitman.[11] In a similar tone, Eliot
confessed of Whitman (in his introduction to *Ezra Pound: Selected Poems*)
that he "had to conquer an aversion to his form as well as to much of
his matter" in order to be able to read him.[12] But in spite of their
obvious distaste for Whitman, neither Pound nor Eliot escaped entirely
the long shadow of the *Leaves*. Pound seemed to recognize this inheritance when he wrote in a brilliant short poem, "I make a pact with
you, Walt Whitman— / . . . It was you that broke the new wood, /
. . . We have one sap and one root."[13] No one deeply read in the *Leaves*
can escape its pervasive feeling and form in pages of Pound's *Cantos*
and Eliot's *Four Quartets*.[14]

Both Eliot and Pound, in rejecting their native culture and settling
abroad, probably remained more American than Whitman who stayed
in Brooklyn and Camden. Eliot was unable to hack himself loose from

his deep Puritan roots, and Pound could not cut himself out of the dense entanglement of political-economic debate over visionary panaceas. Whitman escaped from the American past in a way these poets could not. By their intense and distorted Americanism they alienated themselves from the epic poet of American democracy.

The tradition with which Whitman is most intimately allied, however, is one that has been largely overshadowed by the Pound-Eliot axis and their wasteland progeny. It is a tradition that transcends national boundaries and literary periods. For want of a better term, it might be called the bardic tradition; and, for some sense of its meaning, the words of Algernon Swinburne might serve. Although Swinburne was later to turn against Whitman, his first rapturous response found expression in his book on William Blake, where he perceptively linked the two in their profoundest natures: "The great American is not a more passionate preacher of sexual or political freedom than the English artist. To each the imperishable form of a possible and universal Republic is equally requisite and adorable as the temporal and spiritual queen of ages as of men. To each all sides and shapes of life are alike acceptable or endurable. From the fresh free ground of either workman nothing is excluded that is not exclusive. The words of either strike deep and run wide and soar high." Even in their shortcomings, Swinburne asserted, they are akin: "their poetry has at once the melody and the laxity of a fitful stormwind; . . . being oceanic, it is troubled with violent ground-swells and sudden perils of ebb and reflux, of shoal and reef, perplexing to the swimmer or the sailor; in a word, . . . it partakes the powers and the faults of elemental and eternal things."[15]

The essence of the bardic tradition is its embodiment of "elemental and eternal things." Whatever Whitman shares with Blake, he got it without borrowing but by drinking from a deep and common spring. Some modern poets who have sipped at that same spring are Hart Crane, D. H. Lawrence, Dylan Thomas, and Allen Ginsberg. All of these poets have been, or have attempted to be, like Whitman, "poets of the kosmos [who] advance through all interpositions and coverings and turmoils and stratagems to first principles" (421). Crane relates most closely to Whitman's epic themes of the American experiment; Lawrence, to the procreative themes of the "mystic deliria"; Thomas, to the bardic themes of primeval wisdom and incantation; and Ginsberg, to the "Calamus" themes of adhesive love and to the wanderlust

longing of the "Song of the Open Road." In spite of wide divergences
of style, these four poets share their high regard for Whitman and his
Leaves.

It was an irony of Crane's fate that he was most severely condemned
(by the wasteland critics) for the allegiance which most fully inflamed
his imagination. The section of his masterpiece, *The Bridge*, which
reveals the allegiance in the form of an ode to Walt, has been repeatedly
cited as the poem's weakest part. This critical view developed in large
part out of deep hostility to Whitman rather than out of objective
examination of Crane's poetry. Some critics have even blamed Crane's
suicide on the Good Gray Poet![16] Crane's lines on Whitman display an
understanding that runs far beyond that of Crane's severest critics:

> Our Meistersinger, thou set breath in steel;
> And it was thou who on the boldest heel
> Stood up and flung the span on even wing
> Of that great Bridge, our Myth, whereof I sing![17]

The imaginative link between Whitman's "Crossing Brooklyn Ferry"
and Crane's *The Bridge* (also Brooklyn's) is direct and deep. Crane was
right—in his instincts against the wasteland tradition—to turn to the
affirmative, connecting, and fusing poetry of Whitman for his primary
alliance. His *The Bridge* was meant to be a major embodiment of America's twentieth-century myth to match the epic embodiment of her
nineteenth-century myth in *Leaves*.

Paralleling Crane's ode to Whitman is D. H. Lawrence's essay on
him in *Studies in Classic American Literature*. Lawrence's feelings about
the American poet were mixed, but the magnetism was too strong to
withstand. Lawrence confessed: "Whitman, the great poet, has meant
so much to me. . . . Ahead of all poets, pioneering into the wilderness
of unopened life, Whitman. Beyond him, none."[18] These assertions in
themselves, in spite of the accompanying reservations, should have
warned Lawrence's critics against such statements as that of F. R.
Leavis about Whitman (*D. H. Lawrence: Novelist*)—"it would be difficult to think of a writer more radically unlike Lawrence."[19] In reality
the kinship of Whitman and Lawrence is profound and extensive. In
describing the nature of his own verse (Preface to *New Poems*), Lawrence
called it the poetry of the "incarnate Now"—a kind, he declared,
whose greatest example was none other than Whitman.[20] But Lawrence's allegiance went beyond his poetry. The major themes of his

novels show the impact of the *Leaves*. He wrote in a letter in 1919: "But I find in [Whitman's] Calamus & Comrades one of the clues to a real solution—the new adjustment."[21] The Calamus theme is thoroughly explored in a number of the novels—in the Cyril Beardsley-George Saxton friendship in *The White Peacock*, in the Rupert Birkin-Gerald Crich friendship in *Women in Love*, and in the Aaron Sisson-Rawson Lilly friendship in *Aaron's Rod*. And like Whitman, Lawrence carried the Calamus theme beyond the personal to the social level, especially in *The Plumed Serpent*. More widely admired, however, is Lawrence's handling of the procreational and sexual themes throughout his work. Whitman's "Children of Adam" is the poetic forerunner embodying this theme. Like Whitman's Adam, Lawrence's characters seem in search of the new Garden, from the early *The Trespasser* through the late *Lady Chatterley's Lover* (found for a time by the lady and the gamekeeper) and *The Man Who Died*.[22]

Those who visited Dylan Thomas in his seaside study in Laugharne recall that the Welsh poet had two portraits pasted above his desk, a large picture of Whitman and a smaller image of Blake.[23] The portraits offer a symbolic statement of the bardic tradition with which Thomas felt strong alliance. The points of affinity between Whitman's *Leaves* and Thomas's poems are many, but perhaps the most immediate in impact is the theme of creative cosmic energy. Like Whitman's, Thomas's sex poems are not love poems but procreational poems that identify the individual with primeval, elemental forces of the universe: "The force that through the green fuse drives the flower / Drives my green age; that blasts the roots of trees / Is my destroyer."[24] More than any other poet Thomas captures the suggestion of the frenzied, frenetic chant and the primitive, magic incantation that marked Whitman at his best. As Swinburne said of Whitman and Blake, Thomas's poetry seems to partake of "the powers and faults of elemental and eternal things." It is difficult to read a poem like "Especially When the October Wind" (with such lines as "The signal grass that tells me all I know," or "By the sea's side hear the dark-vowelled birds") without recalling the *Leaves* and particularly such poems as "Out of the Cradle Endlessly Rocking."[25]

It is doubtful that Whitman, were he alive today, would be satisfied that his call for a race of bards had been fulfilled. He would recognize Crane, Lawrence, and Thomas as vital imaginative and spiritual heirs. But he would see that his prediction of the 1855 Preface ("There will soon be no more priests. . . . A superior breed shall take their place . . . the gangs of kosmos and prophets en masse shall take their place" [425]) had not come to pass. And for his comment to today's America, perhaps he would merely point to what he had once written in *Democratic Vistas*: "Our fundamental want to-day in the United States, with closest, amplest reference to present conditions, and to the future, is of a class, and the clear idea of a class, of native authors, literatuses, far different, far higher in grade than any yet known, sacerdotal, modern, fit to cope with our occasions, lands, permeating the whole mass of American mentality, taste, belief, breathing into it a new breath of life, giving it decision" (457).

An Original American Poetry: The Lyric Epic

On reviewing a new Whitman biography in 1981, Howard Moss wrote: "Certain writers belong not only to the history of literature but to history itself, and Whitman is one of them. He was crucially positioned: The American colonies declared their independence exactly forty-three years before his birth, in 1819, and the Revolution was still a vivid event in the minds of adults around him. Psychically, his life stretched from the Revolution through the Civil War to the era of the robber barons. Truly an American poet of change. . . . Whitman was several men in one: Brahmin, bohemian, spokesman for a new democratic society, dandy, creator of an original kind of American poetry— a self-educated and self-intoxicated peasant of the ecstatic."[26]

What, essentially, is Whitman's "original kind of American poetry"? In a little noted paragraph in "A Backward Glance," Whitman confessed being indebted to Edgar Allan Poe, not to his poetry but to his prose: "I was repaid in Poe's prose by the idea that (at any rate for our occasions, our day) there can be no such thing as a long poem. The same thought had been haunting my mind before, but Poe's argument, though short, work'd the sum and proved it to me" (450). Whitman's confession may seem strange, coming as it does from the poet of that greatest of all American long poems, *Leaves of Grass*. But in effect, what Poe did for Whitman was to enable him to see how to write his long poem without violating "psychal necessity"—that is, by making the long poem out of a sequence of subtly related lyric moments, each of which could hold the attention of the reader through a sitting or session of reading.

Shortly after expressing his appreciation to Poe in "A Backward Glance," Whitman turned to the strategies he settled on many decades before, when he was about to set out on his epic work: "Another point had an early settlement, clearing the ground greatly, I saw, from the time my enterprise and questionings positively shaped themselves (how best can I express my own distinctive era and surroundings, America, Democracy?) that the trunk and centre whence the answer was to radiate, and to which all should return from straying however far a distance, must be an identical body and soul, a personality—which personality, after many considerations and ponderings I deliberately settled should be myself—indeed could not be any other" (450).

It appears clear from the beginning, at least as Whitman remembered that beginning in old age, that Whitman's ambition was epic, and that he had to invent a new epic form for the new era and the new country. Poe gave him the clue for his basic structure of a *lyric epic,* and out of his strong instinct he concluded that his own personality must be the "trunk and centre" of an enterprise that was to express his time and his country, America and democracy.

The measure of Whitman's success in his epic enterprise may be gauged by the grudging tribute paid him by Ezra Pound in a 1909 essay entitled "What I Feel about Walt Whitman": "Mentally I am a Walt Whitman who has learned to wear a collar and a dress shirt (although at times inimical to both). Personally I might be very glad to conceal my relationship to my spiritual father and brag about my more congenial ancestry—Dante, Shakespeare, Theocritus, Villon, but the descent is a bit difficult to establish. And, to be frank, Whitman is to my fatherland (*Patrium quam odi et amo* [the Fatherland I love and hate so much] for no uncertain reasons) what Dante is to Italy and I at my best can only be a strife for a renaissance in America of all the lost or temporarily mislaid beauty, truth, valor, glory of Greece, Italy, England and all the rest of it."[27]

It is difficult to think of many major American poets who have not felt, like Pound, the need to produce their own long poem—and who have not felt that Whitman was looking over their shoulder as they wrote. And the long poems produced have, in the main, had the characteristics that Whitman brought together for the first time in *Leaves of Grass*: the form of the *lyric epic,* in which the smaller units are connected to the whole poem not through a continuing narrative within the poem but rather through a single sensibility—the poet's Personality—that lies behind and filters through them all. Thus the poem's structure reflects the contours of the poet's mind; the poem takes on the shape of a life, the configuration of a time.

Like Whitman, these other poets have seen themselves as the "age transfigured," and they have come to say with Whitman: "O I see flashing that this America is only you and me" (250). Thus by delving into themselves as lyric poets they have reached (or tried to reach), in the profounder or communal depths, the epic dimension of their enterprise. It is interesting that most of these poets who have written long poems have spoken of their work, at some point or other, as epic in form. In *The American Quest for a Supreme Fiction: Whitman's Legacy in the Personal Epic* (1979),[28] I have argued that Whitman is the preeminent epic poet of America. But there is no reason to deny America a number of epic poets—or even anti-epic poets. It would certainly fit Whitman's notion of the ideal American democracy that it embrace not one but a number of epic poets. The examples I have dealt with in my book are Ezra Pound's *Cantos* (1917–72), T. S. Eliot's *The Waste Land* (1922), William Carlos Williams's *Paterson* (1946–58), Hart Crane's *The Bridge* (1930), Charles Olson's *Maximus Poems* (1953–68, 1978), John Berryman's *Dream Songs* (1964–69), and Allen Ginsberg's *The Fall of America: Poems of These States* (1973).

But there are innumerable other examples available, from Louis Zukofsky's ambitious and demanding *A* (1927–79) to A. R. Ammons's readable and rambling "disposable epic," *Tape for the Turn of a Year* (1965), written on a single roll of adding-machine tape. It appears that the form is adaptable and resilient, and will attract many more poets before its potential is exhausted. In short, it looks as though Whitman's haunting figure will remain a presence in American literature; he will be lurking there, waiting to see if the "poets to come" live up to his expectations expressed in the "Inscriptions" poem addressed to them:

I myself but write one or two indicative words for the future,
I but advance a moment only to wheel and hurry back in the darkness.

I am a man who, sauntering along without fully stopping, turns a casual
        look upon you and then averts his face,
Leaving it to you to prove and define it,
Expecting the main things from you.

(13)

Notes and References

Preface

1. See William White, "Editions of *Leaves of Grass*: How Many?" *Walt Whitman Review* 19 (1973): 111.

Chapter One: The Masks of Whitman

1. Numbers in parentheses following Whitman quotations refer to pages in *Walt Whitman; Complete Poetry and Selected Prose,* ed. James E. Miller, Jr. (Boston: Houghton Mifflin, Riverside Edition A34, 1959).

2. One book, Esther Shephard's *Walt Whitman's Pose* (New York: Harcourt, Brace & Co., 1938), is devoted to Whitman's various self-created images. The book is persuasive in its thesis that Whitman is indebted for his conception of the vagabond poet to George Sand's epilogue to *The Countess of Rudolstadt.* The work is marred, however, by its tone of indignation and by its failure to distinguish between deliberate fakery and genuine drama.

3. The definitive treatment of the shaping influence of opera on Whitman's poetry is Robert D. Faner, *Walt Whitman and Opera* (Philadelphia: University of Pennsylvania Press, 1951).

4. This myth of Whitman's Creole romance in New Orleans appears as early as Bliss Perry, *Walt Whitman: His Life and Work* (New York: Houghton Mifflin, 1906). It was perpetuated by succeeding biographers. Whitman's own exaggeration of the length and nature of his New Orleans experience, implicit in his approval of the lifetime biographies (particularly Richard M. Bucke's *Walt Whitman* [Philadelphia: David McKay, 1883]), lent an air of importance and mystery that made the myth believable.

5. Perry, *Walt Whitman: His Life and Work,* 256.

6. "Walt Whitman and His Poems" in Horace L. Traubel, Richard Maurice Bucke, and Thomas B. Harned, eds., *In Re Walt Whitman* (Philadelphia: David McKay, 1893), 13.

7. Ibid., 14.

8. "*Leaves of Grass*: A Volume of Poems Just Published" in Traubel, *In Re Walt Whitman,* 25.

9. Ibid.

10. A useful treatment of Whitman and phrenology is Edward Hungerford, "Walt Whitman and His Chart of Bumps," *American Literature* 2 (1931): 350–84.

11. "Leaves of Grass," in Traubel, *In Re Walt Whitman,* 25.

12. William Dean Howells, *Literary Friends and Acquaintances* (New York: Harper & Brothers, 1901), 74.

13. The factual and mythical connections between Whitman and Lincoln are thoroughly explored in William Eleazar Barton, *Abraham Lincoln and Walt Whitman* (Indianapolis: Bobbs-Merrill, 1928). Whitman's Lincoln poems may be profitably compared with James Russell Lowell's tribute in "Ode Recited at the Harvard Commemoration"; Whitman's *Drum-Taps* may similarly be compared and contrasted with Herman Melville's Civil War poems in *Battle-Pieces and Aspects of the War* (1866).

14. There has been much speculation about the conscious and unconscious psychological relationship between Whitman and Doyle. The volume of letters written to Doyle between 1868 and 1880, published as *Calamus,* ed. Richard Maurice Bucke (Boston: Laurens Maynard, 1897), and later published in *The Complete Writings of Walt Whitman,* ed. Richard M. Bucke, Thomas B. Harned, and Horace L. Traubel (New York: G. P. Putnam's Sons, 1902), contains an introduction outlining an interview in which Doyle told Whitman's literary executors, "I never knew a case of Walt's being bothered up by a woman" (*The Complete Writings,* 8:7). The tone of the letters is ardent and intense, suggesting ambivalent and turbulent emotions. Although modern psychology might well call the absolute innocence of the relationship into question, there is no clear-cut evidence that the more ambiguous and less spiritual feelings and impulses ever became manifest or overt.

15. Here the ellipses are mine, but Whitman often used ellipses (or dots) for rhetorical purposes. In order to avoid cluttering his texts, I have not tried to indicate each such use.

16. The article that Rossetti encouraged Anne Gilchrist to make out of the commentary on Whitman in a number of her letters was entitled "An Englishwoman's Estimate of Walt Whitman" and appeared in the *Boston Radical,* May 1870; it was reprinted in *In Re Walt Whitman,* 41–55. An illuminating and touching record of Mrs. Gilchrist's proposal and Whitman's gentle rejection is preserved in *The Letters of Anne Gilchrist and Walt Whitman,* ed. Thomas B. Harned (New York: Doubleday, Doran & Co., 1918).

Chapter Two: Growth of the Leaves

1. *Leaves of Grass* (Brooklyn: Fowler & Wells, 1856), 345–46. Appropriately called the most important letter in American literature, Emerson's praise, though extravagant, strikes a genuine note that is persuasive.

2. *The Uncollected Poetry and Prose of Walt Whitman,* ed. Emory Holloway (Garden City, N. Y.: Doubleday, Page & Co., 1921), 1:10.

3. *Leaves of Grass by Walt Whitman: Inclusive Edition,* ed. Emory Holloway (Garden City, N. Y.: Doubleday, Page & Co., 1926), 558.

4. *The Complete Writings,* 4:28.

5. Ibid., 4: 16–17.

6. Ibid., 6:104.

7. For a study of the oral sources of Whitman's poetry, see C. Carroll Hollis, *Language and Style in "Leaves of Grass"* (Baton Rouge: Louisiana State University Press, 1983).

8. Whitman's letter to Symonds is quoted in Gay Wilson Allen, *The Solitary Singer: A Critical Biography of Walt Whitman* (New York: Macmillan, 1955), 535.

9. See Emory Holloway, *Free and Lonesome Love: The Secret of Walt Whitman* (New York: Vantage Press, 1960), with its frontispiece of a picture of a boy who Holloway takes to be "Son of Walt Whitman."

10. See *The Memoirs of John Addington Symonds: The Secret Homosexual Life of a Leading Nineteenth-Century Man of Letters*, ed. Phyllis Grosskurth (New York: Random House, 1984); for two psychoanalytical commentaries on Whitman's response to Symonds's letter and other implications of the "Calamus" poems, see Edwin Haviland Miller, *Walt Whitman's Poetry: A Psychological Journey* (New York: New York University Press, 1968), and Stephen A. Black, *Whitman's Journeys into Chaos: A Psychoanalytical Study of the Poetic Process* (Princeton: Princeton University Press, 1975); also see part 2 of *Walt Whitman: Here and Now*, ed. Joann P. Krieg (Westport Conn.: Greenwood Press, 1985), and "Coda: English Readers of Whitman," in Eve Kosofsky Sedgwick, *Between Men: English Literature and Male Homosexual Desire* (New York: Columbia University Press, 1985).

11. See especially Justin Kaplan, *Walt Whitman: A Life* (New York: Simon & Schuster, 1980); Harold Aspiz, *Walt Whitman and the Body Beautiful* (Urbana: University of Illinois Press, 1980); Paul Zweig, *Walt Whitman: The Making of a Poet* (New York: Basic Books, 1984); and Charley Shively, ed., *Calamus Lovers: Walt Whitman's Working-Class Camerados* (San Francisco: Gay Sunshine Press, 1987).

12. *Walt Whitman's "Leaves of Grass": The First (1855) Edition*, ed. Malcom Cowley (New York: Viking Press, 1959), 48; the dots are Whitman's in his first edition; they do not represent ellipses.

13. Ibid., 145.

14. Ibid., 48.

15. *Leaves of Grass* (1856), 346.

16. Ibid.

17. Ibid., 356.

18. In a letter to Harrison Blake (7 December 1856), Thoreau wrote: "That Walt Whitman, of whom I wrote to you, is the most interesting fact to me at present. I have just read his 2nd edition (which he gave me) and it has done me more good than any reading for a long time. Perhaps I remember best the poem of Walt Whitman an American & the Sun Down Poem. There are 2 or 3 pieces in the book which are disagreeable to say the least, simply sensual. He does not celebrate love at all. It is as if the beasts spoke. I think that men have not been ashamed of themselves without reason. No doubt,

there have always been dens where such deeds were unblushingly recited, and it is no merit to compete with their inhabitants. But even on this side, he has spoken more truth than any American or modern that I know. I have found his poem exhilirating encouraging. As for its sensuality,—& it may turn out to be less sensual than it appeared" (*The Correspondence of Henry David Thoreau*, ed. Carl Bode and Walter Harding [New York: New York University Press, 1958], 444–45).

19. Whitman described the incident: "During those two hours he was the talker and I the listener. It was an argument-statement, reconnoitring, review, attack, and pressing home (like an army corps in order, artillery, cavalry, infantry), of all that could be said against that part (and a main part) in the construction of my poems, 'Children of Adam.' More precious than gold to me that dissertion [sic]—it afforded me, ever after, this strange and paradoxical lesson: each point of E.'s statement was unanswerable, no judge's charge ever more complete or convincing, I could never hear the points better put—and then I felt down in my soul the clear and unmistakable conviction to disobey all and pursue my own way" (*The Complete Writings*, 5:26–27).

20. In *William Blake* (*The Complete Works of Algernon Charles Swinburne* [New York: Gabriel Wells, 1926], 16: 342–43), Swinburne thought Whitman and Blake so much alike that there might be some reason to "preach the transition of souls or transfusion of spirits. . . . The words of either strike deep and run wide and soar high." In *Songs Before Sunrise* (1871) (*The Complete Works*, 2:184–88), Swinburne wrote a poem "To Walt Whitman in America" asking for a "song oversea for us." But later, in *Studies in Prose and Poetry* (*The Complete Works*, 15: 316), Swinburne devoted an essay ("Whitmania") to attacking Whitman: "But Mr. Whitman's Eve is a drunken apple-woman, indecently sprawling in the slush and garbage of the gutter amid the rotten refuse of her overturned fruit-stall."

Chapter Three: A Poetics for Democracy

1. Two valuable treatments of closely related topics are Norman Foerster, *American Criticism* (Boston: Houghton Mifflin, 1928), and Maurice O. Johnson, *Walt Whitman as a Critic of Literature* (Lincoln: University of Nebraska Press, 1938).

2. For a valuable analysis of metaphors that have dominated literary theory in different ages, see M. H. Abrams, *The Mirror and the Lamp: Romantic Theory and the Critical Tradition* (New York: Oxford University Press, 1953).

3. An excellent contrast in views toward science is provided by section 23 of "Song of Myself" ("Hurrah for positive science! long live exact demonstration!" [41]) and Edgar Allan Poe's sonnet of indictment, "To Science."

4. The epithets have seemed so apt as to become titles of books: Joseph

Beaver, *Walt Whitman—Poet of Science* (New York: King's Crown Press, 1951), and Hugh I'Anson Fausset, *Walt Whitman: Poet of Democracy* (New Haven: Yale University Press, 1942).

5. See, for example, George B. Hutchinson, *The Ecstatic Whitman: Literary Shamanism and the Crisis of the Union* (Columbus: Ohio State University Press, 1986).

6. "Leaves of Grass," in Traubel, *In Re Walt Whitman*, 24.

7. *The Complete Writings*, 5:40.

8. Yvor Winters, for example, blames all of Hart Crane's artistic failures and even his suicide on Whitman. And amazingly enough, Winters "proves" his novel thesis not by quoting Whitman but by quoting Emerson, on the naïve assumption that the one may be equated with the other. In reality, Winters oversimplifies Whitman's thought in order to attack it. See "The Significance of *The Bridge*, by Hart Crane, or What Are We to Think of Professor X?" *In Defense of Reason* (New York: Alan Swallow, 1947), and particularly the definition of Whitman's central theory: "In life and in art the automatic man, the unreflective creature of impulse, is the ideal; he is one with God and will achieve the good life and great art" (578). Whitman's poetics are a great deal more complex and subtle than this statement would suggest.

9. *The Collected Writings of Walt Whitman*, ed. Gay Wilson Allen and Scully Bradley, *The Correspondence of Walt Whitman: 1842–1867*, vol. 1, ed. Edwin H. Miller (New York: New York University Press, 1961), 246.

10. *The Complete Writings*, 5:40.

11. Ralph Waldo Emerson, "The Poet," *Essays: Second Series* (Boston: Houghton Mifflin, 1888), 15.

12. Quoted in Horace Traubel, ed., *An American Primer* (Boston: Small, Maynard Co., 1904), viii–ix.

13. "Slang in America" was reprinted in *The Complete Writings*, 6: 149–57. Traubel, ed., *An American Primer*.

14. *The Complete Writings*, 6: 150.

15. Traubel, *In Re Walt Whitman*, 27.

16. Ibid., 24.

17. Ibid.

Chapter Four: The Structure of the Leaves

1. Other proposals for the structure of *Leaves of Grass* appear in William Sloane Kennedy, *Reminiscences of Walt Whitman* (London: Alexander Gardner, 1896), 100–2; Irving Story, "The Structural Pattern of *Leaves of Grass*," *Pacific University Bulletin* 38, no. 38 (January 1942): 2–12; and Thomas Edward Crawley, *The Structure of "Leaves of Grass"* (Austin: University of Texas Press,

1970). For a thorough and detailed discussion of the structure of *Leaves of Grass,* see James E. Miller, Jr., *A Critical Guide to "Leaves of Grass"* (Chicago: University of Chicago Press, 1957), 163–255.

2. See "Hardy and Well-Defined Women" in Aspiz, *Walt Whitman and the Body Beautiful,* and C. Carroll Hollis, "Reviews" (of Joann P. Kreig, ed., *Walt Whitman: Here and Now,* and Eve Kosofsky Sedgwick, *Between Men: English Literature and Male Homosexual Desire*), in *Walt Whitman Quarterly Review* 3, no. 4 (Spring 1986): 31–38.

3. To argue that Whitman's revision of his 1855 prose Preface into poetry proves that his poetry is really just rearranged prose is to overlook the possibility that he may have written poetry to begin with—and merely arranged it in the paragraphs of prose. Indeed, William Everson (a poet himself) has successfully arranged the whole of the 1855 Preface as poetry and published it under the title *American Bard, by Walt Whitman: The Original Preface to "Leaves of Grass" Arranged in Verse* (New York: Viking Press, 1982).

Chapter Five: The Individual Leaves

1. There is no need to bring forth an array of critics in an attempt to demonstrate critical unanimity on Whitman's poetry. Any list of the great poems made by any individual critic will vary a bit from the list presented here. But my strong impression, which derives not only from wide reading in Whitman criticism but also from detailed observation of Whitman poems included in numerous poetry anthologies, is that by and large the Whitman canon of select poems is fairly standardized.

2. The structure proposed here should be compared with two others that have been formulated. In "The Structure of Walt Whitman's "Song of Myself,'" *English Journal* (college ed.) 27 (September 1938):597–607, Carl F. Strauch suggested the following grouping: 1. Paragraphs 1–18, the Self; mystical interpenetration of the Self with all life and experience; 2. Paragraphs 19–25, definition of the Self; identification with the degraded, and transfiguration of it; final merit of Self withheld; silence; end of the first half; 3. Paragraphs 26–38, life flowing in upon Self, then evolutionary interpenetration of life; 4. Paragraphs 39–41, the Superman; 5. Paragraphs 42–52, larger questions of life—religion, faith, God, death; immortality and happiness mystically affirmed.

In his edition of the 1855 *Leaves,* Malcolm Cowley defined the structure of the poem primarily in terms of Indian philosophy: first sequence (chants 1–4): the poet or hero introduced to his audience; second sequence (chant 5): the ecstasy; third sequence (chants 6–19): the grass; fourth sequence (chants 20–25): the poet in person; fifth sequence (chants 26–29): ecstasy through the senses; sixth sequence (chants 30–38): the power of identification; seventh sequence (chants 39–41): the superman; eighth sequence (chants 42–50): the sermon; ninth sequence (chants 51–52): the poet's farewell.

For a review of critical comments on the structure of "Song of Myself," see Gay Wilson Allen, *The New Walt Whitman Handbook,* (New York: New York University Press, 1986), 73–77.

3. Both Richard M. Bucke, in his *Cosmic Consciousness* (New York: E. P. Dutton, 1923 [215–37]), and William James, in his *Varieties of Religious Experience* (New York: Longmans, Green, 1902 [395–96]), express their belief that Whitman actually underwent some kind of mystical experience that is specifically the basis for "Song of Myself," particularly section 5. For a fuller treatment of Whitman's mysticism, see chapter 8.

4. Evelyn Underhill, *Mysticism: A Study in the Nature and Development of Man's Spiritual Consciousness* (London: Methuen, 1926). See footnote 3, above, for James, *Varieties of Religious Experience.* James assigns to Whitman the "sporadic" type of mystical experience, characterized by its trance-like state and its spiritual and physical exhaustion; see chapter 8. Evelyn Underhill traces in detail the successive distinctive stages of the mystic as he struggles toward his goal of Union with the Transcendent. Although she does not mention Whitman, her definitions of the various stages of the Mystic Way seem relevant to "Song of Myself."

5. For a full and extended analysis of the poem as defined by this structure, see Miller, *A Critical Guide to "Leaves of Grass,"* 6–35.

6. *The Uncollected Poetry and Prose,* 2: 93.

Chapter Six: Recurring Images

1. Quoted in William Sloane Kennedy, *The Fight of a Book for the World* (West Yarmouth, Mass.: Stonecroft Press, 1926), 177.

2. Sigmund Freud, "Symbolism in Dreams," *A General Introduction to Psychoanalysis,* trans. Joan Riviere (New York: Liveright Publishing Corporation, 1935), 143: "Birth is regularly expressed [in dreams] by some connection with water: we are plunging into or emerging from water, that is to say, we give birth or are being born."

3. The water image in T. S. Eliot, particularly in *The Waste Land,* seems almost invariably to represent fertility. In Whitman, although the suggestion of fertility is frequently present, the fertility-meaning is by no means the primary content of the symbol. One element that encompasses most of the water's meanings in *Leaves of Grass* is time. The sea (as in "Out of the Cradle Endlessly Rocking") may be not only the realm of spirituality, but also the embodiment of eternity, where all time goes. Rivers, streams, rivulets (as in "Crossing Brooklyn Ferry" and "Autumn Rivulets") are *time passing*; and, when they have finally run into the sea, they have become eternity. Lakes and ponds (as in "By Blue Ontario's Shore" and "Calamus") are *time arrested* or *time present*; as the ocean is associated with spiritual achievement after death, the bodies of inland waters represent spiritual achievements in life; if the ocean bestows insight into death, the inland waters bestow insight into life. Whit-

man utilizes the water image as fertility symbol in the "pent-up" river-figure in "Children of Adam." But this figure is primarily a figure of time, as the poet himself suggested in "A Woman Waits for Me": "Through you I drain the pent-up rivers of myself, / In you I wrap a thousand onward years" (77).

4. These three major themes may be related to the basic three-part structure of *Leaves of Grass* as outlined at the end of chapter 4, "The Structure of the *Leaves*."

5. See Fredson Bowers, "Whitman's Manuscripts for the Original 'Calamus' Poems," *Studies in Bibliography* 6 (1953): 257–65. See also the discussion of Whitman's manuscripts prepared between the 1856 and 1860 editions in Allen, *The Solitary Singer*, 221–28.

Chapter Seven: Language and Wit

1. See chapter 3, footnote 12.

2. The language of *Leaves of Grass* is subjected to analysis in two articles by Louise Pound: "Walt Whitman and the French Language," *American Speech* 1 (May 1926): 421–30; "Walt Whitman's Neologisms," *American Mercury* 4 (February 1925): 199–201. The latter article concludes (201): "In vocabulary, . . . except for his peculiar reliance upon foreign loan-words, he [Whitman] better illustrates the taste of the Twentieth Century than that of the Nineteenth." A large part of F. O. Matthiessen's treatment of Whitman in *American Renaissance* (New York: Oxford University Press, 1941) is devoted to *Leaves of Grass* as a language experiment. See especially pp. 517–625. The most scholarly and comprehensive analysis of Whitman's language is Hollis, *Language and Style in "Leaves of Grass."*

3. Ezra Pound has stated: "From an examination of Walt made twelve years ago the present writer carried away the impression that there are thirty well-written pages of Whitman; he is now unable to find them" (*ABC of Reading* [Norfolk, Conn: New Directions Publishing Corp., 1934], 192). This somewhat flippant statement is modified by succeeding qualifying statements ("Whitman's faults are superficial"), but the tenor of the criticism remains unchanged. Pound advises: "The only way to enjoy Whitman thoroughly is to concentrate on his fundamental meaning. If you insist, however, on dissecting his language you will probably find that it is wrong *NOT* because he broke all of what were considered in his days 'the rules' but because he is spasmodically conforming to this, that or the other; sporadically dragging in a bit of 'regular' metre, using a bit of literary language, and putting his adjectives where, in the spoken tongue, they are not." In spite of these shortcomings, however, Pound implies that Whitman did occasionally succeed: "His real writing occurs when he gets free of all this barbed wire." Randall Jarrell, in "Some Lines from Whitman," presents persuasively a point of view opposite to Pound's. Jarrell asks, "Can Whitman really be a sort of Thomas Wolfe or Carl Sandburg or Robinson Jeffers or Henry Miller—or a

sort of Balzac of poetry, whose every part is crude but whose whole is somehow great? He is not, nor could he be; a poem, like Pope's spider, 'lives along the line,' and all the dead lines in the world will not make one live poem" (*Poetry and the Age* [New York: Alfred A. Knopf, 1953], 113–14).

4. See chapter 2, footnote 1.

5. See chapter 3, footnote 14.

Chapter Eight: The Bardic Voice

1. Henry Adams, *The Education of Henry Adams* (Boston: Houghton Mifflin, 1918), 385.

2. I offer extended treatment of Whitman and Lawrence later in this chapter.

3. If we apply Sigmund Freud's dream symbols to an interpretation of the symbolic imagery of *Leaves of Grass,* we discover some interesting meanings. We may note in Freud ("Symbolism in Dreams," *A General Introduction to Psychoanalysis,* 140) that "the symbolic representation of onanism . . . by *pulling off a branch* is very typical." Note "I Saw in Louisiana a Live-Oak Growing": "And I broke off a twig with a certain number of leaves upon it, and twined around it a little moss, / And brought it away, and I have placed it in sight in my room" (93). Or we may note, again in Freud (141), that the "*act of mounting . . .* stairs is indubitably symbolic of sexual intercourse." See "Song of Myself": "My feet strike an apex of the apices of the stairs, / On every step bunches of ages, and larger bunches between the steps" (62). Again Freud (138): ". . . dreams of flying . . . must be interpreted as dreams of general sexual excitement, dreams of erection." Frequently in *Leaves of Grass* the poet seems to be flying through the air with the speed of a comet: "Speeding through space, speeding through heaven and the stars, / Speeding amid the seven satellites and the broad ring, and the diameter of eighty thousand miles" (50). Freud (139): "The female genitalia are symbolically represented by all such objects as share with them the property of enclosing a space or are capable of acting as receptacles. . . . *doors and gates* represent the genital opening." See Whitman: "I see the elder hand pressing reviving supporting, / I recline by the sills of the exquisite flexible doors, / And mark the outlet, and mark the relief and escape" (67).

According to C. G. Jung ("On the Relation of Analytical Psychology to Poetic Art," *Contributions to Analytical Psychology,* trans. H. G. and Cary F. Baynes [New York: Harcourt Brace & Co., 1928], 245), there are two unconsciouses, the most significant of which is the *collective unconscious*—"the primordial contents of which are the common heritage of mankind." The collective unconscious contributes to the poetic work (246) the "primordial image or archetype . . . essentially . . . a mythological figure." It is the contribution of the frequently unrecognized symbols of the collective unconscious that makes a work of art great. But there is also the *personal unconscious.* Jung said (245), "From this sphere art also receives tributaries, dark and turbid though they be; but if they become a major factor they make the work of art a symptomatic rather than a symbolical product." By making this distinction, Jung was able to avoid Freud's tendency to see art and neurosis as synonymous (227): "a healthy human reason must assuredly revolt at the notion of artwork and neurosis being placed in the same category." Citing examples that seem in every instance applicable to Whitman, Jung asserts (228): "That one poet is influenced more by the relation to the father, another by the tie to the mother, while a third reveals unmistakable traces of repressed sexuality in his works—all this can be said equally well not only of every neurotic, but also of every normal human being. Hence nothing specific is thereby gained for the judgment of a work of art."

In the final analysis, it is perhaps impossible to say whether Whitman's sexual imagery derives from one unconscious or the other—or, indeed, from higher levels of consciousness. Whatever the source, Whitman seemed aware throughout his career of the pervasiveness—and purposefulness—of his sexual imagery. In many of his poems, such as "The Sleepers," he may be seen not so much as an example of Freud's thesis but as a forerunner of Freud's theory.

4. James, *Varieties of Religious Experience,* 380–81.

5. Ralph Waldo Emerson, "The American Scholar," *Emerson's Complete Works* (Cambridge: Riverside Press, 1883), 1:104.

6. *The Correspondence of Henry David Thoreau,* 445.

7. W. D. O'Connor, *The Good Gray Poet* (New York: Bunce and Huntington, 1866), 30.

8. John Burroughs, *Notes on Walt Whitman as Poet and Person* (New York: J. S. Redfield, 1871), 45.

9. Bucke, *Cosmic Consciousness,* 215–37.

10. James, *Varieties of Religious Experience,* 395.

11. See chapter 7, footnote 3.

12. T. S. Eliot, Introduction, *Ezra Pound: Selected Poems* (London: Faber & Gwyer, 1928), 8.

13. Ezra Pound, "A Pact," *Ezra Pound: Selected Poems,* 97.

14. For Whitman-Pound relationships, see Herbert Bergman, "Ezra Pound and Walt Whitman," *American Literature* 27 (1955): 56–61, which prints Pound's essay "What I Feel about Walt Whitman" for the first time. For Whitman-Eliot relationships see S. Musgrove, *T. S. Eliot and Walt Whitman* (Wellington: University of New Zealand Press, 1952), and James E. Miller, Jr., "Whitman and Eliot: The Poetry of Mysticism," *Quests Surd and Absurd: Essays in American Literature* (Chicago: University of Chicago Press, 1967), 112–36.

15. Swinburne, *William Blake, The Complete Works,* 16: 342–44.

16. See Allen Tate, "Hart Crane," *Collected Essays* (Denver: Alan Swallow, 1959), 225–37, and Yvor Winters, "The Significance of *The Bridge* by

Hart Crane, or What Are We to Think of Professor X?" *In Defense of Reason.* See also chapter 3, footnote 8.

17. Hart Crane, "The Bridge," *The Collected Poems of Hart Crane* (New York: Liveright Publishing Corporation, 1946), 38.

18. D. H. Lawrence, *Studies in Classic American Literature* (New York: Boni and Liveright, 1930), 171. See entire last chapter, "Whitman."

19. F. R. Leavis, *D. H. Lawrence: Novelist* (New York: Alfred A. Knopf, 1956), x.

20. D. H. Lawrence, Preface, *New Poems* (New York: B. W. Huebsch, 1920), v.

21. Quoted in Edward Nehls, ed., *D. H. Lawrence: A Composite Biography* (Madison: University of Wisconsin Press, 1957), 1: 500–1.

22. For a full treatment of the Whitman-Lawrence relationship, see James E. Miller, Jr., Bernice Slote, and Karl Shapiro, *Start with the Sun* (Lincoln: University of Nebraska Press, 1960), part 2, 57–134.

23. Bill Read, "A Visit to Laugharne" in John Malcom Brinnin, ed., *A Casebook on Dylan Thomas* (New York: Thomas Y. Crowell, 1960), 270.

24. Dylan Thomas, *Collected Poems 1934–1952* (London: J. M. Dent, 1952), 9.

25. See Miller, Slote, Shapiro, *Start with the Sun,* part 4, 169–90, for a discussion of the Whitman-Thomas relationship.

26. Howard Moss, "A Candidate for the Future," *New Yorker,* 14 September 1981, 184.

27. Ezra Pound, "What I Feel about Walt Whitman," *Selected Prose: 1909–1965,* ed. William Cookson (New York: New Directions Publishing Corp., 1973), 145–46.

28. James E. Miller, Jr., *The American Quest for a Supreme Fiction: Whitman's Legacy in the Personal Epic* (Chicago: University of Chicago Press, 1979).

Selected Bibliography

PRIMARY WORKS

Editions

Editions of *Leaves of Grass* appeared in 1855, 1856, 1860, 1867, 1871, and 1881; reprintings from existing plates were issued in 1876, 1889, and 1891–92 (see chapter 2). Editions recently reprinted and available include: Malcolm Cowley, ed., *Walt Whitman's "Leaves of Grass": The First (1855) Edition* (New York: Viking Press, 1959); Roy Harvey Pearce, *"Leaves of Grass" by Walt Whitman: Facsimile Edition of the 1860 Text* (Ithaca, N. Y.: Cornell University Press, 1961).

Working editions of *Leaves*: Malcolm Cowley, ed., *The Complete Poetry and Prose of Walt Whitman* (New York: Pellegrini & Cudahy, 1948), 2 vols.; Emory Holloway, ed., *Inclusive Edition: "Leaves of Grass"* (New York: Doubleday & Company, 1926); James E. Miller, Jr., *Walt Whitman: Complete Poetry and Selected Prose,* paperback (Boston: Houghton Mifflin, 1959); Sculley Bradley, and Harold W. Blodgett, *Walt Whitman: "Leaves of Grass"* (New York: W. W. Norton, 1973).

The Complete Writings of Walt Whitman. Edited by Richard M. Bucke, Thomas B. Harned, and Horace L. Traubel. New York: G. P. Putnam's Sons, 1902. 10 vols.

The Collected Writings of Walt Whitman. General Editors, Gay Wilson Allen and Sculley Bradley. New York University Press, 1963–.

The Correspondence. 6 vols. Edited by Edwin H. Miller. 1961–1977.

Daybooks and Notebooks. 3 vols. Edited by William White. 1978.

The Early Poems and the Fiction. Edited by Thomas Brasher. 1963.

"Leaves of Grass": Comprehensive Reader's Edition. Edited by Harold Blodgett and Sculley Bradley. 1965.

"Leaves of Grass": A Textual Variorum of the Printed Poems. 3 vols. Edited by Sculley Bradley et al. 1980.

Notebooks and Unpublished Prose Manuscripts. 6 vols. Edited by Edward F. Grier, 1984.

Prose Works 1892. 2 vols. Edited by Floyd Stoval. 1963–64.

Manuscripts and Miscellaneous Writings

American Bard, by Walt Whitman: The Original Preface to "Leaves of Grass" Arranged in Verse. Arranged by William Everson. New York: Viking Press, 1982.

An American Primer. Edited by Horace Traubel. Boston: Small, Maynard & Co., 1904. Reissued with an afterword by Gay Wilson Allen. Stevens Point, Wis.: Holy Cow! Press, 1987.

Calamus. Edited by Richard Maurice Bucke. Boston: Laurens Maynard, 1897. Letters to Peter Doyle written 1868–80.

Civil War Letters of George Washington Whitman. Edited by Jerome Loving. Introduction by Gay Wilson Allen. Durham, N. C.: Duke University Press, 1975. Valuable primary materials.

Dear Brother Walt: Letters of Thomas Jefferson Whitman. Edited by Dennis Berthold and Kenneth Price. Kent, Ohio: Kent State University Press, 1985. Valuable primary source materials.

Faint Clews and Indirections: The Manuscripts of Walt Whitman and His Family. Edited by Clarence Cohdes and Rollo G. Silver. Durham, N. C.: Duke University Press, 1949.

The Gathering of the Forces. Edited by Cleveland Rodgers and John Black. New York: G. P. Putnam's Sons, 1920. 2 vols. Material from Brooklyn *Daily Eagle*, 1846–47.

The Half-Breed and Other Stories. Edited by Thomas Ollive Mabbott. New York: Columbia University Press, 1927. Five short stories.

I Sit and Look Out. Edited by Emory Holloway and Vernolian Schwarz. New York: Columbia University Press, 1932. Editorials from the Brooklyn *Daily Times,* 1857–59.

In Re Walt Whitman. Edited by Horace L. Traubel, Richard Maurice Bucke, and Thomas B. Harned. Philadelphia: David McKay, 1893. A memorial volume containing tributes and some Whitman materials, such as the 1855 reviews.

The Letters of Anne Gilchrist and Walt Whitman. Edited by Thomas B. Harned. New York: Doubleday, Doran & Co., 1918. Letters of a love affair that never materialized.

New York Dissected. Edited by Emory Holloway and Ralph Adimari. New York: R. R. Wilson, 1936. Articles from *Life Illustrated,* 1855–56.

The Uncollected Poetry and Prose of Walt Whitman. Edited by Emory Holloway. Garden City, N. Y.: Doubleday, Page & Co., 1921. 2 vols. Early poems and prose, manuscripts, notebooks, and novel, *Franklin Evans, or The Inebriate.*

Walt Whitman and the Civil War. Edited by Charles I. Glicksberg. Philadelphia: University of Pennsylvania Press, 1933. A collection of articles and manuscripts.

Walt Whitman Looks at the Schools. Edited by Florence Bernstein Freedman. New York: King's Crown Press, 1950. Articles on education from Brooklyn *Evening Star* and the Brooklyn *Daily Eagle.*

Walt Whitman of the New York "Aurora": Editor at Twenty-Two. Edited by Joseph Jay Rubin and Charles H. Brown. State College, Pa.: Bold Eagle Press, 1950. Articles from the New York *Aurora,* 1842.

Walt Whitman's Workshop. Edited by Clifton Joseph Furness. Cambridge: Harvard University Press, 1928. Notes for lectures and manuscripts for essays and introductions to the *Leaves.*

Whitman's Manuscripts: "Leaves of Grass" (1860). Edited by Fredson Bowers. Chicago: University of Chicago Press, 1955. Contains important manuscripts for the "Calamus" and other sections.

With Walt Whitman in Camden. Horace Traubel. Vol. 1: *March 28–July 14, 1888.* Boston: Small, Maynard & Co., 1906. Vol. 2: *July 16–October 31, 1888.* New York: Appleton & Co., 1908. Vol. 3: *November 1, 1888–January 20, 1889.* New York: Mitchell Kennerly, 1914. Vol. 4: *January 21–April 7, 1889.* Philadelphia: University of Pennsylvania Press, 1953. Vol. 5: *April 8–September 14, 1889.* Carbondale: Southern Illinois University Press, 1964. Vol. 6: *15 September 1889 to 6 July 1890.* Carbondale: Southern Illinois University Press, 1982. Invaluable source for Whitman's recorded conversations.

The Wound-Dresser. Edited by Richard Maurice Bucke. Boston: Small, Maynard & Co., 1898. Letters written from the hospitals in Washington, D.C., during the Civil War.

SECONDARY WORKS

Studies

Allen, Gay Wilson. *The New Walt Whitman Handbook.* New York: New York University Press, 1975 (updated 1986). Replaces *Walt Whitman Handbook* (Chicago: Packard & Company, 1946). Indispensable for the serious student of Whitman

————. *A Reader's Guide to Walt Whitman.* New York: Farrar, Straus & Giroux, 1970. A good introduction.

————. *The Solitary Singer: A Critical Biography of Walt Whitman.* New York: Macmillan, 1955; revised edition, New York: New York University Press, 1967; reprinted with 1984 Preface, Chicago: University of Chicago Press, 1985. The most detailed and probably the definitive biography.

————. *Walt Whitman, as Man, Poet, and Legend.* Carbondale: Southern Illinois University Press, 1961. Contains key essays on Whitman by long-time Whitman critic, Allen.

————, ed. *Walt Whitman Abroad.* Syracuse, N. Y.: Syracuse University Press, 1955. Translations of criticism from Germany, France, Scandinavia, Russia, Italy, Spain and Latin America, Israel, Japan, and India.

Arvin, Newton. *Whitman.* New York: Macmillan, 1938. Stresses political, economic views of Whitman.

Aspiz, Harold. *Walt Whitman and the Body Beautiful.* Urbana: University of Illinois Press, 1980. Explores relation of Whitman's poetry to nineteenth-century pseudoscience.

Asselineau, Roger. *The Evolution of Walt Whitman: The Creation of a Personality.* Cambridge: The Belknap Press of Harvard University, 1960. *The Evolution of Walt Whitman: The Creation of a Book.* Cambridge: The Belknap Press of Harvard University, 1962. Originally published as *L'Evolution de Walt Whitman: Après la première édition des Feuilles d'herbe.* Paris: Didier, 1954. A useful and interesting treatment from the French perspective.

Bailey, John Cann. *Walt Whitman.* New York: Macmillan, 1926. A brief and general early treatment that is still useful.

Barrus, Clara. *Whitman and Burroughs, Comrades.* New York: Houghton Mifflin, 1931. Valuable as a source for many documents.

Barton, William Eleazar. *Abraham Lincoln and Walt Whitman.* Indianapolis: Bobbs-Merrill, 1928. Exhausts the possibilities on this interesting topic.

Bazalgette, Leon. *Walt Whitman, the Man and His Work.* Garden City, N. Y.: Doubleday, Page & Co., 1920. An early French view; still useful.

Beaver, Joseph. *Walt Whitman—Poet of Science.* New York: King's Crown Press, 1951. A valuable critical study.

Black, Stephen A. *Whitman's Journeys into Chaos: A Psychoanalytical Study of the Poetic Process.* Princeton, N. J.: Princeton University Press, 1975. Focuses on the poetry as revelation of Whitman's emotional problems.

Blodgett, Harold. *Walt Whitman in England.* London: Oxford University Press, 1934. Comprehensive treatment of Whitman's reputation in England.

Bloom, Harold. "The Central Man: Emerson, Whitman, Wallace Stevens." In *The Ringers in the Tower.* Chicago: University of Chicago Press, 1971. Useful in placing Whitman in relation to poets who come before and after.

Briggs, Arthur E. *Walt Whitman: Thinker and Artist.* New York: Philosophical Library, 1952. Emphasizes Whitman's philosophy.

Broderick, John C., ed. *Whitman the Poet.* Belmont, Calif.: Wadsworth, 1962. A useful collection of critical essays.

Bucke, R. M. *Walt Whitman.* Philadelphia: David McKay, 1883. An early biography that Whitman helped to shape.

———. *Cosmic Consciousness.* New York: E. P. Dutton & Co., 1901. Brilliant, erratic, perhaps wild—but provocative: a study of Whitman and other mystics.

Cady, Edwin H., and Louis J. Budd, eds. *On Whitman: The Best from "American Literature."* Durham, N. C.: Duke University Press, 1987. Valuable collection of useful commentary on Whitman's work.

Canby, Henry Seidel. *Walt Whitman, an American.* Boston: Houghton Mifflin, 1943. Stresses democratic element in Whitman.

Cavitch, David. *My Soul and I: The Inner Life of Walt Whitman.* Boston: Beacon Press, 1985. Provocative Freudian examination of the poetry in the context of family relationships.

Chari, V. K. *Walt Whitman in the Light of Vedantic Mysticism.* Lincoln: University of Nebraska Press, 1964. Authoritative reading of the poetry in the light of the mystical doctrines of the Upanishads of Hinduism.

Chase, Richard. *Walt Whitman Reconsidered.* New York: William Sloane Associates, 1955. An unusual and stimulating approach, particularly in its analysis of "Song of Myself" as a comic poem.

Coyle, William, ed. *The Poet and the President: Whitman's Lincoln Poems.* New York: Odyssey Press, 1962. Contains the poems and a large number of commentaries.

Crawley, Thomas Edward. *The Structure of "Leaves of Grass."* Austin: University of Texas Press, 1970. An attempt to find the structure of the whole of *Leaves of Grass.*

De Selincourt, Basil. *Walt Whitman: A Critical Study.* New York: Mitchell Kennerley, 1914. A pioneer critical study still of value.

Eby, Edwin Harold. *A Concordance of Walt Whitman's "Leaves of Grass" and Selected Prose Writings.* Seattle: University of Washington Press, 1949–54. An invaluable research aid.

Eitner, Walter H. *Walt Whitman's Western Jaunt.* Lawrence: University of Kansas Press, 1981. Useful biographical material.

Erkkila, Betsy. *Walt Whitman among the French.* Princeton: Princeton University Press, 1980. Important account of Whitman's influence in France.

Faner, Robert D. *Walt Whitman and Opera.* Philadelphia: University of Pennsylvania Press, 1951; reprint, Carbondale: Southern Illinois University Press, Arcturus Books, 1972. An excellent demonstration of how opera shaped Whitman's poetry.

Foerster, Norman. *American Criticism.* Boston: Houghton Mifflin, 1928. A review of critical principles of major American writers, including Whitman.

Grosskurth, Phyllis, ed. *The Memoirs of John Addington Symonds: The Secret Homosexual Life of a Leading Nineteenth-Century Man of Letters.* New York: Random House, 1984. Important background for the Symonds-Whitman correspondence.

Hindus, Milton, ed. *Leaves of Grass One Hundred Years After.* Stanford: Stanford University Press, 1955. Includes important essays by Hindus, William Carlos Williams, Richard Chase, Leslie Fiedler, Kenneth Burke, David Daiches, John M. Murray.

Hollis, C. Carroll. *Language and Style in "Leaves of Grass."* Baton Rouge: Louisiana State University Press, 1983. Valuable application of linguistic and speech-act theory to the poetry.

Holloway, Emory. *Whitman: An Interpretation in Narrative.* New York: Alfred A. Knopf, 1926. A thoroughly informed study that remains eminently readable.

————. *Free and Lonesome Heart: The Secret of Walt Whitman.* New York: Vantage Press, 1960. Claims to have discovered identity of Whitman's son.

Hutchinson, George B. *The Ecstatic Whitman: Literary Shamanism and the Crisis of the Union.* Columbus: Ohio State University Press, 1986. Emphasizes Whitman as a priestlike shaman playing a public role.

Jaén, Didier Tisdel. *Homage to Walt Whitman: A Collection of Poems in Spanish, with English Translations and Notes.* English foreword by Jorge Luis Borges. University: University of Alabama Press, 1969. Invaluable collection, revealing Whitman's impact especially in Latin America.

Jarrell, Randall. "Some Lines from Whitman." In *Poetry and the Age.* New York: Alfred A. Knopf, 1953. An important, perceptive criticism by a poet.

Johnson, Maurice O. *Walt Whitman as a Critic of Literature.* Lincoln: University of Nebraska Press, 1938. Summarizes Whitman's critical opinions.

Kaplan, Justin. *Walt Whitman: A Life.* New York: Simon & Schuster, 1980. Popular, readable biography.

Kennedy, William Sloane. *The Fight of a Book for the World.* West Yarmouth, Mass.: Stonecroft Press, 1926. An early handbook of historical interest.

Krieg, Joann P, ed. *Walt Whitman: Here and Now.* Westport, Conn.: Greenwood Press, 1985. Collects important essays delivered at a 125th-anniversary conference on *Leaves of Grass.*

Lawrence, D. H. *Studies in Classic American Literature.* New York: Albert Boni, 1923. Offbeat, daring, and brilliant.

Lewis, R. W. B., ed. *The Presence of Walt Whitman.* New York: Columbia University Press, 1962. Treats both the direct and indirect influence of Whitman on successor poets.

Loving, Jerome. *Emerson, Whitman and the American Muse.* Chapel Hill: University of North Carolina Press, 1982. Excellent exploration of the Emerson-Whitman relationship.

Marki, Ivan. *The Trial of the Poet: An Interpretation of the First Edition of "Leaves of Grass."* New York: Columbia University Press, 1976. A defense of the first edition as the best.

Masters, Edgar Lee. *Whitman.* New York: Charles Scribner's Sons, 1937. A pedestrian but competent biography.

Matthiessen, Francis Otto. *American Renaissance.* New York: Oxford University Press, 1941. A pioneer study of America's mid-nineteenth-century writers, including Whitman.

Mendelson, Maurice. *Life and Work of Walt Whitman: A Soviet View.* Moscow: Progress Publishers, 1976. Important account of Whitman's impact in Russia.

Middlebrook, Diane Wood. *Walt Whitman and Wallace Stevens.* Ithaca, N. Y.:

Cornell University Press, 1974. Valuable exploration of connections between two poets so apparently different.

Miller, Edwin H. *Walt Whitman's Poetry: A Psychological Journey.* New York:
New York University Press, 1968. A tactful psychoanalytical reading
that respects the poetry.

————, ed. *A Century of Whitman Criticism.* Bloomington: University of Indiana Press, 1969. Excellent and useful collection.

Miller, James E., Jr. *The American Quest for a Supreme Fiction: Whitman's Legacy
in the Personal Epic.* Chicago: University of Chicago Press, 1979. Account
of successor poets (Pound, Eliot, Crane, Williams, Berryman, and others)
who took over Whitman's innovative form—the personal epic.

————. *A Critical Guide to "Leaves of Grass."* Chicago: University of Chicago
Press, 1957. Critical analyses of the important poems and analysis of the
structure of the whole *Leaves.*

————. "Whitman and Eliot: The Poetry of Mysticism." In *Quests Surd and
Absurd: Essays in American Literature.* Chicago: University of Chicago
Press, 1967. Focuses on the relationship of "Song of Myself" and *Four
Quartets.*

Miller, James E., Jr., Bernice Slote, and Karl Shapiro. *Start with the Sun.*
Lincoln: University of Nebraska Press, 1960. A study of the Whitman
tradition with emphasis on Hart Crane, D. H. Lawrence, and Dylan
Thomas.

Moss, Howard. "A Candidate for the Future." New Yorker, 14 September
1981. An excellent review essay emphasizing Whitman's historical
importance.

Musgrove, S. T. S. *Eliot and Walt Whitman.* Wellington: New Zealand University Press, 1952. A persuasive argument that the relationship is deeper
than usually believed.

Noyes, Carleton Eldredge. *An Approach to Walt Whitman.* New York: Houghton Mifflin, 1910. An enthusiastic early appraisal.

Pearce, Roy Harvey, ed. *Whitman: A Collection of Critical Essays.* Englewood
Cliffs, N. J.: Prentice-Hall, 1962. Emphasizes new perspectives on the
poet.

Perlman, Jim, Ed Folsom, and Dan Campion, eds. *Walt Whitman: The Measure
of His Song.* Minneapolis: Holy Cow! Press, 1981. Invaluable collection
of comments, prose and poetry, on Whitman by fellow poets and other
writers.

Perry, Bliss. *Walt Whitman: His Life and Work.* New York: Houghton Mifflin,
1906. A perceptive, highly readable brief work.

Pound, Ezra. "What I Feel about Walt Whitman." In *Selected Prose: 1909–
1965.* Edited by William Cookson. New York: New Directions Books,
1973. An extraordinary "love-hate" tribute.

Santayana, George. "The Poetry of Barbarism." In *Interpretations of Poetry and
Religion.* New York: Charles Scribner's Sons, 1900. Whitman's primitiv-
ism stressed.

Schyberg, Frederik. *Walt Whitman,* translated by Evie Allison Allen. 1933; New York: Columbia University Press, 1951. Valuable detailed treatment of the various editions.

Sedgwick, Eve Kosofsky. "Coda: English Readers of Whitman." In *Between Men: English Literature and Male Homosexual Desire.* New York: Columbia University Press, 1985. An exploration of Whitman's psychosexual impact on British male readers.

Shephard, Esther. *Walt Whitman's Pose.* New York: Harcourt, Brace & Co., 1938. An eccentric but stimulating study of Whitman's "pose."

Shively, Charley, ed. *Calamus Lovers: Walt Whitman's Working-Class Camerados.* San Francisco: Gay Sunshine Press, 1987. Focus on the homosexual appeal in the "Calamus" cluster of poems.

Stovall, Floyd. *The Foreground of "Leaves of Grass."* Charlottesville: University of Virginia Press, 1974. An important historical-biographical study.

Symonds, John Addington. *Walt Whitman: A Study.* London: John C. Nimms, 1893. A personal testimonial valuable as sensitive, impressionistic criticism.

Thomas, M. Wynn. *The Lunar Light of Whitman's Poetry.* Cambridge: Harvard University Press, 1987. A reading of Whitman's poems (including some usually neglected) in illuminating historical context.

Waskow, Howard. *Whitman: Explorations in Form.* Chicago: University of Chicago Press, 1966. Close reading of individual poems as discrete examples of particular forms.

White, William. *1980: "Leaves of Grass" at 125: Eight Essays.* Detroit: Wayne State University Press, 1980. A variety of essays, some quite valuable.

———, ed. *The Bicentennial of Walt Whitman: Essays from the "Long-Islander."* Detroit: Wayne State University Press, 1976. Various useful essays brought together.

White, William, and Ed Folsom, eds. *Walt Whitman Quarterly Review.* Iowa City: Department of English, University of Iowa. Appears four times a year.

Willard, Charles B. *Whitman's American Fame.* Providence, R. I.: Brown University Press, 1950. Excellent reference work tracing Whitman's reputation after his death in 1892.

Woodress, James, ed. *Critical Essays on Walt Whitman.* Boston: G. K. Hall, 1983. Useful collection of pieces by Whitman critics and scholars.

Zweig, Paul. *Walt Whitman: The Making of the Poet.* New York: Basic Books, 1984. A highly readable and sensitive biography by a poet.

Bibliographies

Allen, Evie Allison. "A Check List of Whitman Publications 1945–1960." In *Walt Whitman as Man, Poet, and Legend,* edited by Gay Wilson Allen. Carbondale: Southern Illinois University Press, 1961.

Allen, Gay Wilson. *The New Walt Whitman Handbook*. New York: New York University Press, 1975 (updated 1986).

American Literary Scholarship: An Annual. Durham, N. C.: Duke University Press, 1963–. Includes a chapter devoted to Whitman.

Asselineau, Roger. "Walt Whitman." In *Eight American Authors: Revised Edition*, edited by James Woodress. New York: W. W. Norton & Co., 1971.

Boswell, Jeanetta. *Walt Whitman and the Critics: A Checklist of Criticism, 1900–1978*. Metuchen, N. J.: Scarecrow Press, 1980.

Giantvalley, Scott. *Walt Whitman, 1838–1939: A Reference Guide*. Boston: G. K. Hall, 1981.

Kummings, Donald D. *Walt Whitman, 1940–1975: A Reference Guide*. Boston: G. K. Hall, 1982.

White, William, and Ed Folsom, eds. *Walt Whitman Quarterly Review*. Iowa City: Department of English, University of Iowa. Appears four times a year and contains an annotated bibliography.

Index